IRISH ARCHITECTURAL AND DECORATIVE STUDIES
Volume III, 2000

IRISH ARCHITECTURAL AND DECORATIVE STUDIES

THE JOURNAL OF THE IRISH GEORGIAN SOCIETY – VOLUME III, 2000

IRISH ARCHITECTURAL AND
DECORATIVE STUDIES
The Journal of the Irish Georgian Society
Volume III, 2000

Published by the Irish Georgian Society
© Irish Georgian Society and the authors,
   2000. All rights reserved.

ISBN 0946846 480

This journal continues the publishing tradition
of the Irish Georgian Society's *Bulletin*
(38 volumes, 1958-1997).

Edited by Dr Seán O'Reilly

Design   John O'Regan (© Gandon)
Production   Nicola Dearey, Gandon
Printing   Betaprint, Dublin
Distribution   Gandon, Kinsale

Produced for the Irish Georgian Society by
Gandon Editions, Oysterhaven, Kinsale
tel +353 (0)21-4770830 / *fax* 021-4770755
e-mail gandon@eircom.net
web-site www.gandon-editions.com

The Irish Georgian Society gratefully acknowl-
edges the grant-aiding of this publication by
J. PAUL GETTY JR. CHARITABLE TRUST
and the support of
MARC FITCH FUND

front cover and flap
The architecture of John Skipton Mulvany
(1813-1870)
cover
Mayfield, Portlaw, Co Waterford
(photographed when still occupied in 1982)
flap, top to bottom
Clodiagh, Portlaw, Co Waterford
Former Meeting House, Clara, Co Offaly
Ballinagore, Newtown, Co Westmeath

back cover and flap
The traditional Irish farmhouse and
cottage garden
cover
The Medlycott Farm, Roundwood, Co Wicklow
flap, top
Box-edged beds of primroses at Maidenhall,
Co Kilkenny
flap, bottom
Daffodils in the apple orchard of the Thomas
cottage, Greenane, near Rathdrum, Co Wicklow

The Irish Georgian Society aims to encourage
an interest in and the preservation of
distinguished examples of architecture and the
allied arts in Ireland.

Further information – and membership
application details – may be obtained from:
IRISH GEORGIAN SOCIETY
74 Merrion Square, Dublin 2
tel +353 (0)1-6767053 / *fax* 01-6620290
e-mail igs@iol.ie

IRISH ARCHITECTURAL AND DECORATIVE STUDIES

THE JOURNAL OF THE IRISH GEORGIAN SOCIETY – VOLUME III, 2000
EDITOR: SEÁN O'REILLY

———

———

———

Shorter Notices

———

—————

Dedicated to
Daniel Gillman

—————

Foreword

THE KNIGHT OF GLIN

THIS IS THE THIRD OF OUR JOURNALS, AND I WOULD LIKE TO TAKE THE OPPORTU-
nity of thanking the J. Paul Getty Jr Charitable Trust and the Marc Fitch
Fund for their invaluable and generous support which has enabled us to
develop and enhance *Irish Architectural and Decorative Studies*. Through the support of the Trust and the Fund, we have been able to publish much more illuminat-
ing material in an extremely attractive format. However, we are still seeking new
research from private scholars and the academic world for future numbers.

This journal discusses cottages and castles, the architect of one of Dublin's
most striking railway stations, and the continuation of the vital index or database of
Ireland's architects from 1720 to 1940.

We are dedicating this journal to Daniel Gillman, himself a descendant of the
Limerick architect William Edward Corbett who designed that local landmark, the
belfry-like 'Tate's Clock'. Daniel has been a pioneer in the collecting of old photographs of Irish buildings, fascinating memorabilia, faded sales catalogues, and all
the ephemera of Ireland's lost world of the 19th and early 20th century. As a private
collection it is unparalleled, and his passionate interest and generosity has infec-
tiously inspired many an Irish scholar and researcher. We are all much in his debt.

Authors' biographies

PATRICK BOWE is an architect, a garden designer and a historian. He is author or co-author of nine books, including three on Irish gardens and *Gardens of Portugal*, *Gardens of Central Europe* and *Gardens of the Caribbean*.

ANA DOLAN is a conservation architect with Dúchas, the Heritage Service. Seven of the twelve churches studied in the research for her article are National Monuments in State care. Her research was undertaken as part of the process of understanding the development of these buildings and their conservation.

FREDERICK O'DWYER is an architect and architectural historian with a particular interest in the nineteenth century. He is the author of *Lost Dublin* (1981), *The Architecture of Deane and Woodward* (1997) and *Irish Hospital Architecture* (1997). He is senior architect in the Architectural Heritage Advisory Service of Dúchas, the Heritage Service.

PETER PEARSON is a historian, campaigner, conservationist and artist. He is a former member of the Heritage Council of Ireland, and has been involved with the restoration of many historic buildings. He is the author of *Between the Mountains and the Sea* (1998) and *The Heart of Dublin* (2000).

ANN MARTHA ROWAN is engaged on the compilation of the database of Irish architects 1720-1940 for the Irish Architectural Archive.

1 – Photographic portrait of John Skipton Mulvany, from A.C. Mulvany's LETTERS
(courtesy Gillman Collection)

Mulvany's signature

The architecture of John Skipton Mulvany (1813-1870)

FREDERICK O'DWYER

THE GREAT CLASSICAL TRADITION OF DUBLIN ARCHITECTURE, BEGUN WITH THE Royal Hospital in the 1680s and brought to a pinnacle with the arrival of James Gandon a century later, did not die with the Act of Union, nor indeed with the ascent of Queen Victoria to the throne. It survived, in the words of Maurice Craig, to 'run out in the sands somewhere between 1860 and 1870'.[1] In the latter year, John Skipton Mulvany, considered by his admirers to have been the Gandon of his age, died at the age of fifty-seven. By the dawn of the twentieth century he had all but been forgotten, until, in 1914, he was, in the words of the late Professor R.M. Butler, rescued 'from oblivion' with the publication of a remarkable book. This was *Monumental Classic Architecture in Great Britain and Ireland during the Eighteenth and Nineteenth Centuries*. It was remarkable in that its author, Professor (later Sir) Albert Richardson, rather than treating the Georgian (then fashionable) and Victorian (decidedly unfashionable) periods separately, described in a continuous narrative the development of the classical tradition from the building of our own Parliament House in College Green in the 1730s up to the works of his own day. As might be expected, Richardson illustrated such notable Dublin buildings as the Casino, City Hall, the Four Courts and the Custom House. That he also included Mulvany's Broadstone Terminus and devoted half a page of eulogistic prose to its author may be as much due to the persuasiveness of his Dublin guide, the same R.M. Butler, as to any prior study of Irish architecture.

Richardson began his piece with the words: 'Ireland has produced many buildings of renown, but few with the genius of J.S. Mulvany.'[2] As late as 1939, in a piece subtitled the 'Last of the Renaissance Architects', Butler described Mulvany (whose name he always spelt with two 'n's) as 'probably the most distinguished architect after the period of [Francis] Johnston and his contemporaries'.[3] For all his polemic Butler never made a detailed study of his hero's career. In the couple of pieces he published he was content merely to quote the rather inadequate list of Mulvany's works printed in his obituary in *The Irish Builder*. In this paper I hope to make good the omission, and place the Broadstone and Mulvany's relatively well-known work for the railway companies in the context of his extensive but almost unknown practice as a house designer and his patronage by a group of interrelated entrepreneurial Quaker families.[4] These clients, many of whom shunned personal publicity and are now largely forgotten, played as vital a role in the Irish economy of the mid-nineteenth century as Gandon's aristocratic patrons had in the closing years of the eighteenth.

FAMILY AND YOUTH

John Skipton Mulvany (Plate 1) was born in 1813, the fourth son of Thomas James Mulvany (1779-1845), a popular artist, and his wife Mary (1779-1865), the daughter of a physician, Dr Cyrus Field. Little is known of the family's origins or of John's upbringing and training. None of his private papers and few of his drawings seem to have survived. The architect's elder brother William, a celebrated mining engineer in the Ruhr, was the subject of a biography (by Kurt Bloemers) published in Germany in 1922.[5] This book was hastily compiled at a difficult time, and is rather inadequate in its treatment of the family: John is mentioned only in the genealogical tree at the start. Bloemers had to rely on papers left by William's daughter Annabella on her death in 1917 when Britain and Germany were at war. The biography was compiled under the terms of her will, which set a time limit for publication. A volume, *Letters from Professor Thomas J. Mulvany RHA to his eldest son William T. Mulvany Esqre...*, which she had privately printed in 1907 (mostly correspondence between her grandfather and father) does contain a couple of references to the young John, as well as a striking photographic portrait of him taken in middle age. The correspondence provides a useful insight into the family circle. According to Annabella Mulvany's introduction to the *Letters*, her grandfather Thomas James Mulvany and his brother John George 'lost their father in early childhood and were brought up by a Roman Catholic bishop'.[6] The name of the prelate is not recorded and the family's origins remain elusive. She appears to confuse him with Dr William Magee, Protestant Archbishop of Dublin, who was a family friend in the 1820s. The future architect was presumably called John after his uncle. The Skiptons were a noted Derry family, possibly friends rather than relatives of the Mulvanys.

Both Thomas James and his brother became professional artists, specialising in landscapes and figure painting, though Thomas initially worked as a miniaturist. Strickland considered him to have been a good draughtsman, 'but his work as a painter was mediocre, though esteemed in his time. He was favourably known as a teacher. He was a man of cultivated taste, with a considerable knowledge of art, and a brilliant conversationalist, which made his society sought after.'[7] Thomas and Mary's first child, William (the future engineer), was born in Sandymount in 1806. The other boys in the family were George Francis, born in Dublin in 1809; Richard Field, born about 1811; John, born in 1813, and Thomas John, born in 1821. There were two girls: Eliza, born in 1807 or 1808, and Mary.

Supporting a large family proved difficult on Thomas's relatively modest income. He was, however, determined to have the best for his children, and used his connections unashamedly to forward their careers. This is particularly apparent from the *Letters*, which indicate the intense, almost obsessional, interest he took in the progress of his eldest son William during his training as a government surveyor, and the often unnecessary and sometimes counterproductive string-pulling he undertook on his behalf.

The Mulvanys seem to have oscillated between the Roman Catholic and Protestant faiths. Thomas appears to have professed the religion of his guardian, while his brother is buried in a Church of Ireland vault. The children were brought up as Catholics. William became a Protestant at the age of sixteen while a student at Dr Wall's Academy in Hume Street, though he was later to marry a Catholic. It is not known whether John was also a pupil at the school, which offered a wide and progressive curriculum.

Thomas James and John George Mulvany were among the founder members of the Royal Hibernian Academy. In 1825 Thomas was appointed first keeper of the Academy House, which had been erected in Lower Abbey Street at the expense of another founder, the architect Francis Johnston. The Mulvany family appear to have resided in a house attached to the premises. Johnston, who had succeeded the painter William Ashford as president of the Academy in 1824, was one of several architects associated with the institution in its early years. Others included Henry Aaron Baker, John Williamson, and Johnston's cousin and associate William Murray. Gandon declined to take an active part, owing to his advanced years, but appeared on the membership list nonetheless. Other leading architects like the Morrisons and the Papworths exhibited annually at the Academy. The eldest Mulvany boy, William, spent a period in Johnston's office in 1824 followed by a year with John Semple, but moved from architecture to surveying with a job at the Ordnance Survey in 1826.[8] From this milieu of artists and architects the young John too developed an interest in architecture. His father had a penchant for Greek classicism. Although an admirer of Gandon, whose *Life* he edited in the 1840s, he thought his use of Roman rather than Greek sources to have been misguided.[9] He arranged for John to be apprenticed to William Deane Butler, a Roman Catholic Dublin-based architect, best remembered today for his classical courthouses and

Gothic churches. He probably began his articles about 1828, at the age of fifteen.

Among the *Letters* can be found a remark made by his father in 1827 that John 'is growing up a fine boy'.[10] Thomas Mulvany moved around the country periodically to undertake commissions. In 1829, for instance, John is mentioned as accompanying other members of the family during a stay in Co Wicklow. At this time his father was working on a painting depicting 'Peasants performing stations at Glendalough'. In April 1833 he wrote, 'John is well nigh to the period of being his own master. In September he will have completed his time with Butler.' He would then have been aged twenty, the apprenticeship probably having been of five years duration. In 1833 also, John exhibited at the RHA for the first time.[11] The work was simply entitled *Design for a Monument*. His address was given as the Academy House. He next exhibited in 1836, giving as his address 24 Upper Sackville Street. His brother George, now embarked on a career in painting, had his studio at the same premises. One of the three designs exhibited on that occasion was a proposal for a new Roman Catholic chapel for the parish of St Mary, Kilkenny. This appears to have been a project for Kilkenny cathedral, which was designed by his former master, William Deane Butler.

ENTERS PRIVATE PRACTICE

On completion of his apprenticeship to Butler in September 1833, Mulvany went into private practice. His earliest known works were for the Dublin and Kingstown Railway and for clients associated with its directors. The railway opened in December 1834 with a terminus near Salthill House, which had been fitted up as an hotel. Mulvany was employed to extend the hotel in 1836. There is no evidence that he executed any designs for the railway company prior to this date. While the elaborate footbridge at Blackrock, constructed by the company for Lord Cloncurry in 1833-34, has been attributed to Mulvany, it is unlikely that he had anything to do with it. At the time it was designed, in the autumn of 1832, Mulvany was still with Butler. A reference in the diary of the company's engineer, Charles Blacker Vignoles, who was delegated to negotiate the right of way with Cloncurry, refers to the bridge having been designed by William Cole junior, architect and county surveyor for Cheshire.[12]

In August 1836, T.J. Mulvany secured a job for his eldest son William with Vignoles through his friendship with the railway magnate James Perry, a director of the Dublin and Kingstown.[13] While the offer of employment was not taken up, it is clear from the *Letters* that Mulvany senior had no personal knowledge of Vignoles, but had enquired about him from another acquaintance, Thomas Bergin, who was

2 – Vault of Peirce Mahony, Mount Jerome Cemetery, Dublin, c.1853
(photo: John Stafford)

3 – Headstone of Robert L. West, Mount Jerome Cemetery, 1850
(photo: John Stafford)

clerk (i.e. secretary) to the company. By this date, the resident engineer Barry D. Gibbons (who also looked after the harbour for the Commissioners of Public Works) had largely taken over from Vignoles, who was based in England.

The origin of the friendship between Mulvany senior and Perry is unknown, but it is clear that this relationship not only launched John into private practice, but introduced him to the coterie of Quaker business families who were his most important patrons. At the RHA summer exhibition of 1836 he exhibited three drawings, one of which, the design for the Kilkenny chapel has already been mentioned. The other two were: 'Villa at Glenageary for Peirce Mahony Esq.' and 'Villa at Killiney – additions now erecting for Alexander Boyle'. Both men were connected with the Dublin and Kingstown Railway company. The RHA exhibition of 1836 opened in May, three months before Mulvany's name first occurs in the company's minute book.[14]

Peirce Mahony (1792-1853) was solicitor to both the Dublin and Kingstown and the Dublin and Drogheda railway companies. Although based in Dublin, he owned estates in Co Kerry and served for a period as MP for Kinsale. In 1836 he was living at one of two new houses he had bought at Gresham Terrace, Kingstown (Dun Laoghaire).[15] The proposed villa at Glenageary seems not to have been built. Mahony subsequently purchased Stillorgan Friary (later known as The Priory), a large neo-Tudor pile built by the Rt Hon A.R. Blake in 1833.

During the 1840s Mahony's law firm had its offices at 22-23 South William Street, the premises of the Pim brothers, who were directors of the D&KR. Mahony's tomb at Mount Jerome (Plate 2) is undoubtedly a Mulvany design, as must be its neighbour, the vault of James Perry, erected in 1844 (fourteen years before Perry's death). The Perry vault looks like a miniature of the Broadstone façade, which it predates. The monument to Robert Lucius West (Plate 3), the portrait painter (d.1850), in the same cemetery is probably also by Mulvany, who would have known him well as an RHA contemporary of his father.

Mulvany's additions to Alexander Boyle's Killiney house, Belle Vue (1836) (Plate 4), are a competent exercise in the classical style he favoured. There is a double-storey top-lit hall, a feature that was to become a hallmark of his houses, though here, unusually, it is circular, in the Gandon tradition. Boyle was a partner in the stockbroking and banking firm of Boyle, Low and Pim. His partner James Pim junior was treasurer (i.e. general manager) of the D&KR.[16] Mulvany appears to have remodelled the adjacent property Glenageary House for another stockbroker, Halliday Bruce, around 1852. This house was demolished in 1978.[17]

Mention has already been made of James Perry (1794-1858) and his friendship with Mulvany senior. Perry, like Pim and a couple of other D&KR directors, was a member of the Society of Friends; the early locomotives on the line were

4 – Belle Vue, Killiney, Co Dublin (1836)
garden front (Irish Architectural Archive)

5 – Royal St George Yacht Club, Dun Laoghaire, Co Dublin (1842-43)
entrance front with the original portico on the right and George Papworth's 1845 replica on the left

sometimes referred to as the 'Quaker engines'. Perry came originally from Rathdowney, Co Laois, where his father, Henry, had a brewery. With his brother Henry, James had established a firm of ironmongers, hardware and iron merchants in Dublin's Pill Lane. He was also a senior partner in the Ringsend Iron Company. He has been described as the 'only genuine proto-tycoon among Irish railway men'.[18] He lived at Obelisk Park, Blackrock. In addition to his directorship of the D&KR, Perry was associated with the launching of the Dublin and Drogheda in 1836, the Great Southern and Western in 1843, the Midland Great Western in 1844, and the Waterford and Limerick in 1845. He was clearly a useful man to know.

Mulvany's first recorded commission from the D&KR, the job of extending the Salthill Hotel, was received in August 1836. The final scheme consisted of some twenty-six extra bedrooms, as well as two gates and a lodge. While the D&KR owned the hotel, it was let out to independent operators, with mixed success. The proposed additions were deferred until 1843 when a consortium, including James Pim, acquired it from the company, thus relieving the D&KR of the financial liability while it continued to enjoy the spin-off in passenger numbers using Salthill station. In the interim, in 1837, Mulvany had designed a new station to serve the hotel, the company's seawater baths, and the now-expanding suburb of Monkstown. The stationhouse, which he extended in 1841, was in the cottage orné style, a rare excursion by Mulvany into the Gothic idiom. The hotel was greatly altered when extended to the designs of John McCurdy in 1865. Both it and the station have been demolished.[19]

Being architect to the line appears to have brought Mulvany numerous commissions from individuals and organisations building in the neighbourhoods opened up by the railway. This was particularly the case in Kingstown, where he had a monopoly on buildings in the harbour area. It may also have been the case in Monkstown, where several terraces and individual villas bear his imprint. In the absence of documentation, however, they can only be regarded as attributions.

Early developments such as Gresham Terrace (1832) at Kingstown and New Brighton/Richmond Hill (1829) at Monkstown were designed by George Papworth. Some of the buildings on Clifton Terrace (begun in the late 1830s) (Plate 9), which includes a variety of house types, are probably by Mulvany.[20] Longford Terrace (1842) (Plate 6), which was let out in individual building lots but with uniform façades, is probably also attributable to him. At the extension to Longford Terrace – a second block begun in the mid-1850s – the roadway is fronted by a robust granite retaining wall (Plate 40), modelled as only Mulvany could. Mulvany probably also designed the two Monkstown developments in which he owned houses: Brighton Vale (begun in 1846) (Plate 7) and Trafalgar Terrace (1844-55) (Plate 8). The latter was built by Daniel Crowe of Pearse Street, Dublin.[21]

6 – Longford Terrace, Monkstown, Co Dublin,
view of the second terrace and the retaining wall of c.1855 (photo: John Stafford)

7 – Brighton Vale, Monkstown, Co Dublin
view of the southern end showing some of the earlier houses (photo: John Stafford)

8 – Trafalgar Terrace, Monkstown, Co Dublin (1844-55)
Mulvany lived on the terrace between 1864 and 1870

Monkstown was also favoured by the various branches of the Pim family who supported the Friends Meeting House there. James Pim junior (1796-1856), the treasurer of the D&KR, was known in the family as 'Imperial James'. Of him it was commented: 'The Railway is the subject of his waking thoughts and nightly dreams ... If he sees that the amusement of the public can be procured by any project, he sees it through the railway glass.'[22] In 1838 Pim acquired Monkstown Castle, a stucco-faced classical house with 'D-ends'. The stone portico *in antis* which he added and extensions to the rear appear to be Mulvany's work (Plate 17). Many of the Monkstown Quakers, Pim included, had purchased houses on the Papworth-designed New Brighton estate in the 1820s.[23]

Mulvany appears to have displaced Papworth to some extent in the locality. Pim planned to open extensive pleasure grounds around Monkstown Castle as a botanical garden, and even tried to tempt the Zoological Society to transfer its collection from the Phoenix Park. Mulvany designed a hilltop observatory in the Grecian style as a centrepiece for the gardens, which were to be laid out by the noted horticulturist Ninian Niven. There was also to be a galleried palm house. Niven published a prospectus in 1839 in which Mulvany is referred to as 'the noted architect', but the project came to nought.[24]

MULVANY'S DUBLIN ADDRESSES

By 1842 Mulvany had moved office to 159 Great Brunswick Street, a premises shared with a coal merchant but near the yards of the leading building firms in the city. The family had by now moved from the Academy House to the suburb of Booterstown. John and George are listed along with their father as residents of Dirker House, Cross Avenue. Of their brothers, William had long been independent and had married in 1832. Richard married in 1841. Thomas John, the youngest, and their sister Mary probably also lived at home, while the other girl, Eliza, resided at Obelisk Park, Blackrock, where she was probably employed as a governess by the Perrys.

In February 1845, Thomas Mulvany died at Dirker House at the age of sixty-five, following what seems to have been a stroke. His children remained on there for a while before dispersing – John to build a house in Monkstown in 1846 and George to get married in 1848. Their mother, who was to survive her husband by over twenty years, appears to have moved in with William. He had risen through the ranks of the public service to become a drainage commissioner. In 1846, with the consolidation of government engineering works into a single department, he became a commissioner for public works.

John's new residence, subsequently described by him in a newspaper adver-

9 – No. 2 Clifton Terrace, Monkstown, Co Dublin (c.1840)
as it was in the 1980s – note the similarity of the plaster decoration to Trafalgar Terrace

tisement as a 'remarkably neat ten-roomed cottage', was situated at Brighton Vale (Plate 10), Seapoint. This was a row of houses laid out on a strip of ground (between the Dublin and Kingstown railway line and the sea) owned by the Lees family and leased to a developer named Christopher Lynch. Mulvany's house seems to have been the present no. 5, a single-storey-over-basement detached cottage, one of a pair with distinctive neoclassical gate piers. Most of the other houses in the row have the Mulvany imprint. Several, of an obviously later date (and similar refaced houses on Crofton Terrace, Dun Laoghaire),[25] are illustrative of his move from simple classicism towards ornate eclecticism in the 1850s. We do not know if Mulvany ever occupied the Brighton Vale house. In August 1848, *Griffith's Valuation* listed it as vacant. Three months later he advertised it for letting or sale in *The Advocate*, a weekly newspaper devoted to railway and business matters lately launched by his brother Richard. Richard and the youngest brother, Thomas John, had hitherto been employed by the Board of Works on famine relief, presumably through William's good offices. In July 1848 John had taken out a lease on an old property called Lakelands, formerly the manor house of Kilmacud, standing on twenty-one acres.[26]

Mulvany's decision to dispose of the Brighton Vale property only two years after signing the lease ties in with his marriage about this time. His bride, Eleanor Burke, was some fourteen years his junior. Little is known of her background. The two families were certainly close, possibly related. The Burke family plot in Mount Jerome had been purchased in 1842 by one Joseph Burke of Cross Avenue for the interment of Kate Burke (possibly his daughter), who had died of consumption, aged seventeen.[27] The architect's brother George signed the burial register. Joseph Burke's name is not listed under Cross Avenue in the street directories; it may well be that he too lived at Dirker House.

The marriage was to be tragically short. Eleanor died of consumption at Lakelands, aged twenty five, on 3 July 1852.[28] Mulvany remained on at the house until 1857 when he disposed of the lease.[29] He next lived at Alma Cottage on Sandycove Avenue South, before moving in 1864 to 4 Trafalgar Terrace, Monkstown, which overlooked his old home on Brighton Vale. All this time he maintained an office in central Dublin, based between 1857 and 1865 at 20 Sackville Street Lower, before he returned to an address on Great Brunswick Street (no. 190).

Mulvany's name also appears in the Dublin directories from 1856 as an auditor of the Royal Hibernian Academy. He was elected an associate of the Academy in 1850, and a full member four years later. He was one of only a few architects to be elected RHA before the introduction of a new charter in 1860. He was less active in the Royal Institute of the Architects of Ireland, founded in 1839, becoming a fellow only after the revival of the organisation in 1864.

*10 – No. 5 Brighton Vale, Seapoint, Co Dublin, built by Mulvany in 1846
– note the characteristic gate piers, probably derived from a J.B. Papworth design*

11 – J.B. Papworth, 'A Park Entrance' from RURAL RESIDENCES *(1818)*
(courtesy Irish Architectural Archive)

12 – Dun Laoghaire (formerly Kingstown) Railway Station, Co Dublin (1839-42)
the channelled masonry of the lower wall surfaces is characteristic of Mulvany's work

13 – Blackrock Railway Station, Co Dublin (1841)
one of several buildings with a portico in antis *feature*

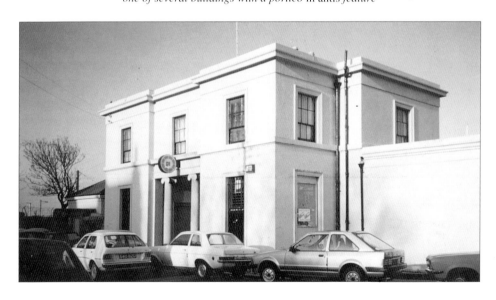

BUILDINGS AT KINGSTOWN HARBOUR

In addition to the Gothic station at Salthill, Mulvany designed Blackrock station (1841) (Plate 13) and the Kingstown terminus, now Dun Laoghaire station (1839-42) (Plate 12).[30] Both replaced earlier, temporary structures, and both were in the classical idiom. Blackrock, a two-storey stucco building, has an Ionic portico *in antis*, a feature that Mulvany was to repeat in numerous designs. The columns are of granite. The contrast between natural stone, as in the portico, and the stucco walls was much favoured by Mulvany. He liked to use cut stone where the budget allowed, but appears to have been averse to leaving brickwork unrendered. At the Kingstown terminus the budget permitted him to specify granite ashlar. Difficulties arose, however, as to the quality of the material. Mulvany compelled the contractor, Samuel Roberts, to remove the stone used in the lower storey. The granite for the basement came from the Murphystown quarry, while that for the upper storey came from Ballyknockan. Both were easier to work than local stone. Here again Mulvany employed an Ionic portico *in antis*.

The treatment of the elevations – rustication to impost height and vertical subdivision by pilasters – was to become a Mulvany hallmark. In 1853-54 the platforms behind the station were roofed over, the ironwork being supplied by Robert Mallet's Victoria Foundry.[31] On the seaward side of the shed, Mulvany designed a remarkable flank wall, executed in granite ashlar. While totally windowless, the wall is extensively modelled, with string courses, pilasters and a massive cornice supported on beautifully worked consoles (Plate 44). The retaining walls of the Broadstone forecourt to Constitution Hill and the aforementioned embankment at Longford Terrace, Monkstown, are similarly detailed. Few Irish architects have brought such plasticity to the detailing of stonework, but precedents for the piers, at least, can be found in engineering works by the Killaly family – for example, the Whitworth Aqueduct (1816-17), Co Longford, by John Killaly (Plate 15), and Monasterevan Aqueduct (1827-28), Co Kildare, by Hamilton Killaly.[32]

Mulvany's second commission in the harbour area came from the Kingstown Boat Club (subsequently renamed the Royal St George Yacht Club) (Plate 5).[33] In April 1842 he was asked to furnish designs for a clubhouse to be erected on a site to the east of the railway station. As with the former, the building had to be kept low (that is, single storey over basement) so as not to obstruct the view enjoyed by the terraces facing the harbour. Funds were limited, precluding the use of stone facings and limiting the external embellishment to a pedimented Ionic portico – again *distyle in antis*. The plan was a simple 'T' with just four main rooms: entrance hall, ballroom, dining room and committee room (with a boat store underneath). Approval was obtained from the ground landlords, the Commissioners of Public

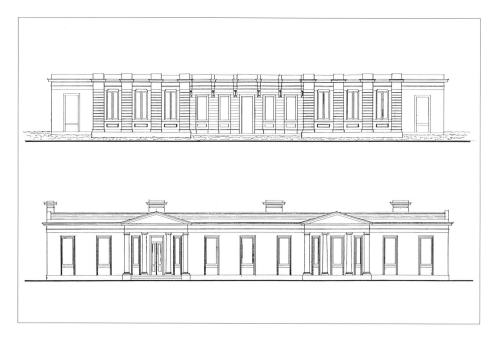

*14 – Royal St George Yacht Club
Dun Laoghaire, Co Dublin
Papworth's elevation of 1844 and
Mulvany's proposed new astylar
elevation of 1848 (top). Sketched
pencil lines on the original
Papworth drawing indicate that
the executed colonnade which
connects the two porticos was an
afterthought.*
(*original drawings in the National
Archives, tracings by the author*)

*15 – Whitworth Aqueduct,
Abbeyshrule, Co Longford
(1816-17), by John Killaly
The baroque modelling of the
stonework, designed to resist the
thrust of water in the aqueduct,
may have inspired some of
Mulvany's retaining walls.*

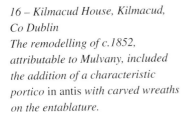

16 – Kilmacud House, Kilmacud, Co Dublin
The remodelling of c.1852, attributable to Mulvany, included the addition of a characteristic portico in antis with carved wreaths on the entablature.

17 – Monkstown Castle, Monkstown, Co Dublin
The house is attributable to George Papworth (c.1829). The Greek Ionic porch, in Portland stone, believed to have been designed by Mulvany, was added c.1838.

Works, and construction completed in 1843 by a local contractor, Edward Masterson. In 1844 it was decided to enlarge the clubhouse by extending it to the west, doubling the façade and replicating the portico as well as adding a wing to the rear. The design was not entrusted to Mulvany, but to George Papworth. Initially Papworth proposed to have the entrance in the new portico, but sensibly relocated it centrally and linked the two projections with a columnar screen.

While Papworth's designs were approved by the committee in January 1845, and built, within four years Mulvany was being asked to alter the façade yet again. His proposal, drawn up in November 1848, called for the elimination of all the columns and pediments, and their replacement by a chaste, if rather severe, astylar elevation with a uniform parapet height. The effect very much relies on modelling, with rusticated pilasters and a recessed entrance loggia without columns (Plate 14). It appears from the drawing that he proposed to support the parapet and roof of the loggia on cast-iron brackets, as he was later to do at Galway Railway Station and the Sailors' Home at Kingstown. This scheme was not executed. The reasons behind the project and its rejection are unclear, but it could hardly have escaped the committee's notice that the new elevation looked uncannily like that designed by Mulvany for another yacht club, the Royal Irish, under construction just a few hundred yards away.

While the membership of the 'George' was largely drawn from the ranks of the Church of Ireland, the promoters of the 'Irish' were an alliance of non-con-

18 – Royal Irish Yacht Club, ground-floor plan from THE BUILDER (1851), redrawn by Maurice Craig (from THE ARCHITECTURE OF IRELAND ... (1982))

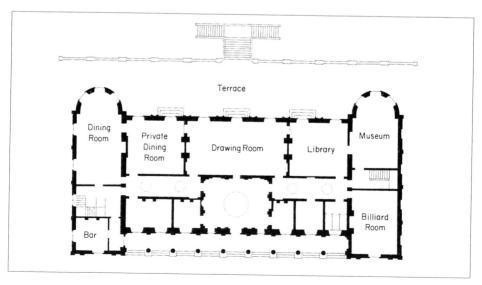

Royal Irish Yacht Club (1847-50), Dun Laoghaire

19 – Nineteenth-century view of entrance front from the north-west (Irish Architectural Archive)

*20 – View of the seaward front
showing the type of nautical balustrade much favoured by Mulvany*

21 – Royal Irish Yacht Club entrance hall
view showing the characteristic Mulvany compartmented ceiling

formists (chiefly Quakers and Huguenots) and Roman Catholics. Among the Quakers was James Pim of the D&KR. The club was founded in July 1846. Mulvany was asked for plans in October, which were approved the following month.[34] Although he was instructed to prepare working drawings in January 1847, the club did not gain possession of the site until the end of the year. In January 1848 tenders were sought for the centre section of the clubhouse, it having been decided to defer building the end sections (with bows on the seaward side) which terminated the nine-bay Ionic colonnaded façade (Plates 19, 20). In the event, the wings were included in the contract and the building was completed in 1850.[35] A more grandiose building than the George, it shares the characteristic of a concealed roof. The plan-form is a double pile, with top-lit central corridors extending on either side of the central hall (Plate 21), which has a decorative coved ceiling. The main enfilade of five rooms (now altered) was on the seaward front (Plate 18). These were the dining room, private dining room, drawing room, library and museum. On the landward side were the main entrance, various offices, bar and billiard room.

Mulvany's last freestanding building in the harbour area was the Sailors' Home or Sailors' Reading Room, one of his last works, exhibited at the RHA in 1868. It stood on Victoria Wharf, on the seaward side of the railway station until its demolition in the 1960s.[36] The design is very much a reprise of the earlier harbour buildings, almost a miniature version of the station, but decorated with paterae, like the Royal Irish.

THE MIDLAND GREAT WESTERN RAILWAY

The second railway line out of the metropolis was the Dublin and Drogheda, begun in 1840 and opened four years later. The Dublin terminus at Amiens Street – by Mulvany's former master William Deane Butler – was completed in 1846. The Great Southern and Western Railway opened their line from Dublin to Carlow in the same year. In March 1845, they advertised in the newspapers for designs for their Dublin terminus at Kingsbridge. Twenty schemes were submitted and passed on to the company's engineer, Sir John Macneill, for assessment.[37] He considered that those submitted by Mulvany, Sancton Wood and Butler, together with a pseudony-mous design entitled *Ireland for Ever*, were of great merit. While both Macneill and the Dublin board of the GSWR placed Mulvany's design at the top of the list, the commission went to Wood, an English architect whose interests appear to have been promoted from the beginning by the company's London committee.

In 1845 the Midland Great Western Railway was incorporated for the establish-ment of a line from Dublin to Mullingar, Longford, Athlone and Galway. Mulvany was appointed company architect at a salary of £250 a year. He held the position until 1850, after which he was remunerated only for specific jobs.[38] Minor buildings were often entrusted to the company engineer, G.W. Hemans. The line followed the route of the Royal Canal, which the company had acquired. At the second half-year-ly meeting of the MGWR board, held in October 1846, it was reported that they had obtained from Mulvany a 'very handsome and suitable design for the terminal sta-tion buildings; but for the present they had not thought it advisable to incur any large expenditure in ornamental buildings or to contract for any part of the design but what they may consider indispensable for the opening of traffic upon the line'.[39]

Some months previously, Mulvany had exhibited at the RHA two drawings of the proposed Dublin terminus at the Broadstone: a south elevation (Plate 18) and a view of the east flank, containing 'Booking Offices, Waiting Rooms etc., now in progress'. The passenger shed, with a roof by the Ballsbridge ironmaster Richard Turner, was also begun at this time (Plate 26). Work on the south elevation – the main front – did not begin until 1850 when a contract was placed with the well-known Dublin builder Gilbert Cockburn. A large plaque on the façade is inscribed 'ERECTED A.D. 1850'. This, the main block, was known as the Directors' House.

The neo-Egyptian monumentality of the Broadstone has been described by Maurice Craig in poetic terms: '...the last building in Dublin to partake of the sub-lime ... the traveller who sees it for the first time, so unexpected in its massive amplitude, feels a little as he might if he were to stumble unawares upon the mon-strous silences of Karnak or Luxor.'[40]

It is difficult to find close precedents for the Broadstone in nineteenth-centu-ry buildings, though Egyptian themes can often be found in funerary architecture. Indeed, the Perry vault at Mount Jerome (Plate 23), erected in 1844 in the form of a miniature temple, contains many of the elements of the Broadstone façade. The common pylon motif may have had its origins in the monumental Egypto-Grec gate piers that became fashionable throughout Ireland from about 1820. The first of these seems to have been erected at Westport House from the designs of J.B. Papworth, based on a plate published by him in *Rural Residences* (1818) (Plate 11).[41] The design was imitated by other architects such as Sir Richard Morrison and John B. Keane; examples may be seen at Fota, Ballyfin, Castlemorres, Harristown and Castle Irvine. Those at two houses near Dublin – Nutley (removed in the 1940s) and Kilruddery – would certainly have been known to Mulvany.

The central pediment of the Broadstone façade is echoed in the architraves of the ground-floor windows. The façade is highly modelled. The horizontal emphasis of the rusticated granite ashlar and string courses is balanced by the subdivision of the wall into a series of vertical planes, treated at parapet level as shallow pedi-ments. The echoing of the main elements in the subsidiary details makes for a har-

22 – Broadstone Railway Station, Dublin terminus of the MGWR from 1846 to 1937 – view of the south elevation (Directors' House), erected in 1850 (photo: Irish Architectural Archive)

23 – Vault of James Perry, Mount Jerome Cemetery – erected in 1844, fourteen years before his death, and six years before the construction of the Directors' House at the Broadstone (photo: John Stafford)

Broadstone Railway Station, Dublin

24 – Detail of the entrance hall at first-floor level (Irish Architectural Archive)

25 – Passenger shed detail (Irish Architectural Archive)

opposite 26 – Site plan (Ordnance Survey 1864-66)

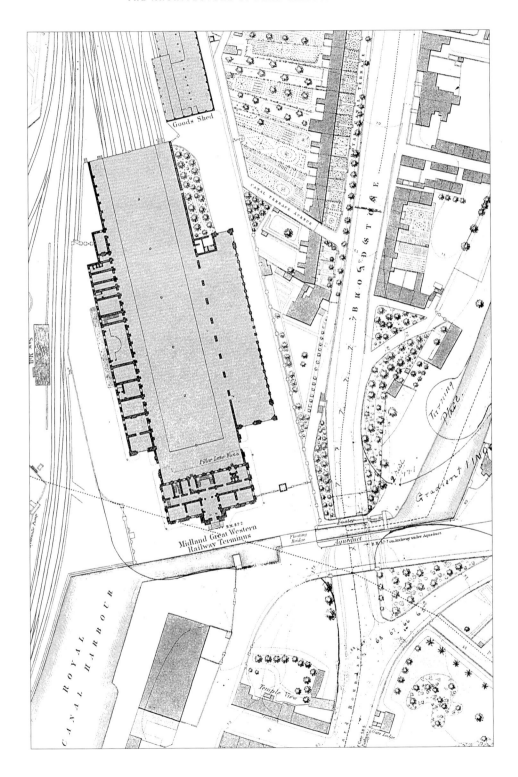

27 – Athlone Railway Station, Co Westmeath (1851)
– a palace façade with five articulated doorways

28 – Pair of houses on the Dunmore Road, Waterford (c.1865), attributable to Mulvany
– note the similarity of the the window surrounds to those at Athlone Station

29 – Galway Hotel and Railway Terminus (1853)
viewed from Eyre Square (photo: Lawrence Collection, National Library of Ireland)

30 – Galway Railway Terminus
photographed in 1982 before the removal of its sash windows

monious composition. Many of the details are neo-Grec, like the carved anthemion and palmette motifs on the entablature and repeated in the entrance lobby. The top-lit hall is subdivided by screens and fluted Doric columns (Plate 24). In stylistic contrast to the façade, the stuccoed back wall of the Directors' House, where it forms the gable of the passenger shed, is replete with Roman neoclassical motifs (Plate 22).

Mulvany also designed the MGWR station at Athlone (Plate 27) (which he exhibited at the RHA in 1851 and 1853) and the terminus and hotel (now the Great Southern) at Galway, exhibited in 1854. Athlone station, built by Cockburns, is finely modelled, with round-headed windows and bold pilasters and consoles.[42] The Galway hotel (Plate 29), built by William Dargan, is unusually bland for a Mulvany design, and, like the terminus itself (Plate 30), has been the subject of some unfortunate modern alterations.[43] Wreaths, a favourite Mulvany motif, are carved on the entablature over the main entrance, perhaps echoing those on the façade of the Broadstone. Among the few surviving internal features is a fine marble fireplace incorporating a pair of bronze discs, emblazoned with the MGWR arms.

At the time the hotel was erected, it was hoped to turn Galway into a major transatlantic port. *The Builder* reported that a group of American capitalists had purchased Mulvany's plans with the intention of erecting a replica in California.[44] The Galway station building, at right angles to and behind the hotel, is a competent design derived from his yacht clubs. The recessed entrance loggia is similar to that proposed for the George Yacht Club in 1848, while the metal balustrade is similar to that at the Royal Irish. The roof of the passenger shed was fabricated by Richard Turner. The station's formal limestone gateway now stands separated from it in the yard of an adjoining fuel depot.

Mulvany was also architect to the Dublin Trunk Connecting Line, a venture with the aim, presumably, of interconnecting the various Dublin termini. This was not eventually achieved until the Loop Line was constructed in 1891.

SOME DUBLIN HOUSES

Among the greatest figures of the Irish railway boom were the contractor William Dargan and the engineer Sir John Macneill. Dargan's experience of Irish railways went back to the Dublin and Kingstown days, while Macneill planned the Dublin and Drogheda, Great Southern and Western, and other lines. Both men appear to have employed Mulvany to redesign their residences.

In the early 1850s Dargan purchased Mount Anville, Co Dublin (Plate 31), former home of Judge Burton. According to the street directories it was first called

Retreat House, Front View – Convent of the Sacred Heart, Mount Anville, Dundrum, Dub

Mount Anville, Goatstown, Co Dublin

31 – The house as remodelled for William Dargan (c.1852-53)
(Irish Architectural Archive)

32 – The entrance gateway in its new position (photo: John Stafford)

33 – Mount Anville, gate lodge (c.1852) (photo: John Stafford, 1988)

34 – Minella, originally Colville, Clonmel, Co Tipperary, gate lodge,
probably the lodge for which Mulvany exhibited a drawing (by Raffles Brown) at the RHA in 1862
– a stucco version of the Mount Anville lodge

Dargan Lodge, then the Tower (when its owner added a belvedere), before reverting to its original name. There can be little doubt that Dargan's improvements, which included the erection of a fine monumental granite gateway and lodge (Plates 32, 33), were designed by Mulvany.[45] Dargan added an Ionic portico *in antis* to the house, using granite blocks of remarkable size. The interior is sumptuous, with a top-lit central hall and adjoining stairhall.

The owner of the property opposite, Mount Anville House (later renamed Knockrabo), appears also to have commissioned his gateway from Mulvany; the stonework is similarly coursed. It is not clear whether the work was commissioned by Robert Orme, who lived there from 1859, or Henry Roe junior, who acquired the property in 1863. Roe greatly extended the house itself, adding a vast double-storey verandah and other features. It is less easy to attribute these to Mulvany. The house was demolished in the early 1980s.

Macneill aggrandised his family home (and birthplace), Mount Pleasant, near Dundalk in Co Louth. Some features, including the staircase, are very Mulvany-like and suggest that he was consulted, though it is probable that many of the concepts, like the full-height portico, were Macneill's own. Macneill has been accredited with the design of a number of railway stations, but appears to have collaborated with architects in most cases.[46] Another figure associated with the Dublin and Drogheda Railway, its solicitor Richard D. Kane, appears to have employed Mulvany to design his Howth residence, Claremont (now the Howth Lodge Hotel) (Plate 35), in 1857. Kane, who succeeded Peirce Mahony at the D&DR, was a member of the Royal Irish Yacht Club. Up until the late 1980s, Claremont retained such typically Mulvany features as a low-pitched roof, with prominent consoles beneath the eaves and bargeboards, and window heads with rounded corners. The tower at Claremont, which escaped the alterations, is capped by a hipped pyramidal roof with dormers and round-headed windows.[47]

A large number of one-off suburban houses can be attributed to Mulvany, though caution must be exercised since some of his former pupils and associates worked in the same style. Shortly after moving to Lakelands, Mulvany had designed a substantial three-storey house, curiously called Hazlewood Cottage (Plate 37), for an adjoining site. It was expensively finished in granite ashlar and punctuated by pilasters, although, by contrast, the interiors were plain. It may have been designed as a speculation: Mulvany exhibited it at the RHA in 1851 as a 'cottage for Henry B. Clarke Esq.' and again in 1853, by which date it had been completed. It was leased to a Captain Maunsell. Kilmacud House nearby (Plate 16) has a fine cut-granite porch decorated with wreaths in the Mulvany style, as well as an imperial staircase. These features were probably added after the property was purchased by Robert Hoey in 1852.[48] The gate lodge, on Kilmacud Road Lower, which had a typi-

35 – Claremont (Howth Lodge Hotel), Howth, Co Dublin (c.1857), photographed c.1982 before the enlargement of the window openings; it was acquired for redevelopment in 1998

36 – Friarsland (now Glenard University Residence), Clonskeagh, Co Dublin, remodelled from an earlier house, Friarland, c.1859, with the rear elevation recast as a façade

cal Mulvany curved roof, was demolished in the 1960s.[49]

Another suburban house exhibited at the RHA (in 1856) was 'a villa in Merrion Avenue, the seat of George MacMullin Esq.'. This can be identified as Glenvar (Plate 58), which had entrances on both Merrion (now Mount Merrion) Avenue and (near the old Mulvany home) on Cross Avenue.[50] It was designed in Mulvany's curved-roof idiom, a picturesque style he often used for villas in contrast to the more ponderous neoclassicism of many of the larger buildings. The eclecticism of his villa architecture was unfavourably commented upon by *The Irish Builder*, which felt that 'it might have been well had he ambitioned other less orthodox styles'.[51]

Substantial suburban villas whose design or alteration are attributable to Mulvany include Newtown House, Blackrock (remodelled c.1850 for William Hodgens); Clonard, Sandyford (1853, for Henry Thompson); Gortmore, Ballinteer (1858, for Richard Atkinson); Friarsland, Roebuck (1859, for Augustus de Butts) (Plate 36), and Montebello, Killiney (1860, for Daniel Connolly) (Plate 40). Smaller houses include three on Churchtown Road (one detached and one pair), while attributable terraces include 31-32 Oakley Road, Ranelagh, 150-153 Rathgar Road, and the block comprising 1 Waterloo Road and 77-79 Upper Leeson Street (Plate 39). A characteristic of these terraces is the concealment of the pitched roofs behind a parapet, as at the Broadstone and the yacht clubs.

Some Mulvany-looking buildings in Dublin are probably by pupils rather than the master, such as Carlisle Terrace (1859-65) on Church Road, Malahide – a row of eight semi-detached houses – which may be by J.J. Lyons (editor of *The Dublin Builder*). On the south side of the city, another one-time assistant Alfred Gresham Jones designed a number of houses in the Mulvany style, including a pair, nos 15 and 16 Avoca Avenue, Blackrock, erected in 1861-63 by a builder named Gregory Murphy.[52] There are other Jones/Mulvany houses on George's Avenue, Blackrock, and at Strand Road and St John's Road, Sandymount.

Jones is not listed among Mulvany's pupils in the *Irish Builder* obituary, but is know to have worked for him in the early 1850s. Three of the perspectives exhibited by Mulvany at the RHA in 1853 were drawn by Jones (the Broadstone, Mullingar Asylum and Hazlewood Cottage). Jones attested the death of the architect's wife, Eleanor Mulvany, in July 1852. Monkstown House, which Jones designed in 1859 (in collaboration with Hugh Carmichael) for the Quaker merchant William Harvey Pim, is very Mulvany-like, but with a tower.[53] Jones, however, had a tendency to over embellish his work, and buildings like the Merrion Hall and the old Wesley College lacked Mulvany's discipline and sense of proportion.[54]

Mulvany's other pupils included John C. Campbell, who joined the Board of Works in 1853, William Farrell, Thomas Mannin and Raffles Brown. Brown execut-

opposite

37 – Hazlewood, Kilmacud,
Co Dublin (1851-53)
(photo: John Stafford)

38 – Athenry Railway Hotel
(later a catering school), Co Galway
(1853-54) – note the characteristic
maritime railings
(photo: Michael Shaughnessy)

39 – Nos 77-79 Upper Leeson Street
and No. 1 Waterloo Road, Dublin –
a formally composed terrace (c.1853)

40 – Montebello, Killiney, Co Dublin
(1860), gates and lodge
Mulvany's typical attention to detail
can be seen in the ironwork

ed a number of perspectives exhibited by Mulvany at the RHA in the early 1860s.[55] Mulvany's last assistant was the watercolourist William Bingham McGuinness, whom he appointed executor of his will.

THE RUHR COALMINES

On 12 May 1853, Dublin's answer to the London Great Exhibition was opened by the lord lieutenant in 'the presence of upwards of 15,000 persons'. The most illustrious visitor during its five-and-a-half month duration was Queen Victoria, who spent several days in Dublin at the end of August. Accompanied by the Prince Consort and the teenage Prince of Wales, she called on the Dargans at the recently completed Mount Anville, and climbed the tower to view the sweep of Dublin Bay.

Another visitor to Dublin that year was Michael Corr van der Maeren, the son of Irish parents who had fled to Belgium following the collapse of Emmet's rising. Corr had lately acquired an estate near the Westphalian town of Gelsenkirchen, and was in search of capital and expertise to investigate its potential as a coal mine. It should be noted that this area, now the heartland of the Ruhr industrial region, was at that time still agricultural and poorly served by roads. It had only recently been connected to the railway system. It seems likely that Corr initially approached Dargan with his proposition. However, having committed himself to underwriting the exhibition to the tune of £100,000 (he eventually lost 'only' £20,000 on the venture), Dargan was hardly in a position to help out financially. James Perry was contacted and expressed interest. The operation was, however, likely to require much more capital than even he could provide. He recommended that his fellow Quaker, the Portlaw industrialist Joseph Malcomson, be brought in on the deal.

Perry had a long-established business relationship with Dargan, going back some twenty years to the building of the Dublin and Kingstown. Malcomson's brother William, who also took a share in the venture, was a major shareholder in the Waterford and Limerick Railway, which Dargan was then completing. Perry had a stake in this line also. Of Ulster-Scots origin, the Malcomsons' principal interests were in corn milling at Clonmel and in cotton spinning at Portlaw. They were also ship owners, and in 1844 had inaugurated a shipbuilding and repair yard in Waterford.[56] They saw in the Ruhr project an opportunity to break the stranglehold of the Welsh coal suppliers on the Irish market. The Irish Quaker entrepreneurs, with their railway and manufacturing interests, were keen to control the price of their raw material.

The Mulvany family were among the immediate beneficiaries of the new venture. William Thomas Mulvany's position as a commissioner of public works had become increasingly shaky in the aftermath of the Rosse committee's inquiry into the operation of land drainage grants in 1852. Richard Griffith, chairman of the commissioners, had long been determined to make Mulvany a scapegoat, and was instrumental in forcing his resignation in June 1853. He had moved to London when he was approached by Corr, Malcomson and Perry with an offer to direct the prospecting operation at Gelsenkirchen. A deal was negotiated whereby William was given a fixed salary and a stake in the venture, with 5% of the profits, though he appears to have been regarded by the promoters as an employee rather than a partner. He moved to Germany in 1854 and opened what was to be the first of three mines, the Hibernia, on St. Patrick's Day, 1856.[57]

Joseph and William Malcomson and Joseph's son David were the main shareholders in this and a second mine, the Shamrock, at Herne, which commenced operation in 1857. Perry's nephews John and James were also shareholders. The enterprise expanded in the 1860s with the acquisition of the Vulcan Ironworks at Duisburg and the sinking of a third mine, the Erin, at Castrop. The youngest of the Mulvany brothers, Thomas John, joined the operation as a colliery manager. It is likely that John Skipton Mulvany also received work from the consortium. We know that his brother erected housing at both the Hibernia and Erin mines. While there is no direct evidence of architectural commissions, it seems more than coincidental that in 1875 his associate, the artist William Bingham McGuinness, exhibited at the RHA a perspective view of houses erected at Castrop for the Prussian Mining Company.

The establishment of the consortium was significant in cementing the relationship between the Mulvany and Malcomson families. In the decade or so following the inauguration of the Ruhr projects, the Malcomsons provided the mainstay of John Skipton Mulvany's architectural practice. There is evidence, however, that the Malcomsons were putting work his way as early as 1851, two years before the Ruhr developments were first mooted. In 1849 Joseph Malcomson had employed the Clonmel architect William Tinsley to aggrandise his home Mayfield, which adjoined the Portlaw mill. Two years later, Tinsley, an ardent Wesleyan who had hitherto enjoyed a successful practice in south-east Munster, decided to emigrate to the United States. His biographer, J.D. Forbes, has suggested that the move may have been partly prompted by what he considered a slight by the Clonmel Quaker community in awarding the design of a Friends' seminary in the town to a 'pretender from Dublin'.[58] It seems certain that the interloper was Mulvany. The building, commissioned in 1846 but converted eighteen years later to a private house known as Prior Park, had a number of stylistic features consistent with his work.[59] It was demolished for a housing development in 1997.

By the end of the 1850s Mulvany was being extensively employed by the

Malcomsons in Clonmel, Portlaw and elsewhere. His first substantial commission from them appears to have been a further enlargement of Mayfield, completed sometime before Joseph Malcomson's death in April 1858.[60] Mulvany exhibited the design at the RHA two months later. He added wings to the house, as well as capping the stuccoed façade with a modelled granite parapet (Plates 41, 42). As Mulvany found it, Mayfield appears to have been a 'long house', one room deep with service accommodation in a rear annex. His first additions were the wings: double pile to the north (with two reception rooms, back to back) (Plates 45, 47); single to the south, with a winter garden. In place of a porch and pair of bay windows (probably added by Tinsley), Mulvany erected a central tower in cut stone, incorporating the entrance porch (Plate 46), and rising to a viewing room above the eaves level. The tower is loosely based on that at Walton House, Surrey, erected in the late 1830s from the designs of Sir Charles Barry. Finally, the service annex was demolished and the house more than doubled in depth, with a top-lit (Georgian-like) central corridor along the spine.

At some point Mulvany must also have aggrandised and enlarged another Malcomson residence in the area, the miller's house at Pouldrew, near Kilmeadan, three miles south-east of Portlaw. The window reveals have his characteristic rounded corners. The flour mill at Pouldrew had been the Malcomsons first venture in

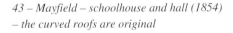

opposite

Mayfield, Portlaw, Co Waterford

*41 – Entrance front in 1982, showing
Mulvany's tower and other embellishments
of the 1850s*

*42 – Entrance front in 1996, showing the
results of vandalism*

*43 – Mayfield – schoolhouse and hall (1854)
– the curved roofs are original*

*44 – Dun Laoghaire (formerly Kingstown)
Railway Station, Co Dublin – flank wall of the
former passenger shed (1853-54). Mulvany's
penchant for brackets is evident here and in the
previous plate.*

Mayfield

45 – Interior of the sitting room, one of two reception rooms in Mulvany's single-storey-over-basement extension to the north of the house (early 20th-century-view) (Poole Collection, National Library of Ireland)

46 – Detail of the porch in 1982

47 – Mayfield
Mulvany's additions appear
to have been the single-
storey-over -basement wings
(reception rooms to the
north (A); conservatory to
the south (B)); tower (C);
and, in a slightly later phase,
the demolition of a service
wing to create a garden
front on the west side with
additional rooms marked (D).
(tracing by the author based on
a survey drawing by T.G. Kiely,
1968, courtesy the late Robert
Jacob)

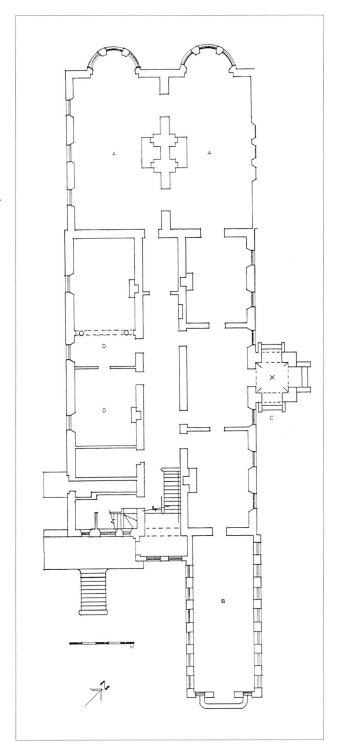

*48 – Clashawaun, Clara, Co Offaly
– pair of houses (late 1860s, much
altered), with a longitudinal
curved roof. The boundary wall is
similar to that at the Clara
Meeting House.*

*49 – Brown Street, Portlaw,
Co Waterford
– terraced houses with transverse
curved roofs. The centre house
here (early 1850s), is one of the
few estate houses in Portlaw with
surviving original sash windows
and decorative eaves.
(photo: Colm Murray)*

east Waterford, being leased by Joseph Malcomson's father, David, in 1824, a year before the family set up in Portlaw. Pouldrew was operated by a younger son, David junior, but as he died in 1840 and the OS map of 1841/42 shows a relatively modest house on the site, the work must postdate him.

Mulvany appears to have had a hand in the the the design of Malcomsons' workers' housing (effectively a rebuilding of the village of Portlaw), constructed between 1850 and 1855, and in the provision of a school and hall in the mill complex itself (Plate 39), erected in 1854.[61] All these buildings have Belfast-truss curved roofs covered with tarred linen produced at the plant (Plate 49). Similar housing was built by the Malcomsons in Co Limerick[62] and by other industrialists in Harold's Cross (Dublin), Carrick-on-Suir, Blarney and Banbridge, and much later, in 1869-74, at Clara (Plate 48). Mulvany was probably architect to at least some of these developments. Mayfield itself also spawned further commissions for grand houses from the Malcomsons in counties Waterford, Tipperary and Dublin. Mulvany exhibited perspectives of each at the RHA.

THE PERRYS, GOODBODYS AND MALCOMSONS

Little has been published on the role of the Quaker entrepreneurs in the Irish economy in the mid-nineteenth century. Many of the families discussed here were interrelated. Undoubtedly there were other business ventures before the Ruhr mines for which Quakers from opposite ends of the country united to fund projects of mutual advantage. Several of the families, for instance, were involved in setting up the Friends' Boarding School in Dublin in 1840, and enterprise that survived just four years.[63] Joseph Malcomson was a subscriber to the school, as was his brother David, the Clonmel mill owner, James and Henry Perry, and Thomas and Jonathan Pim. The school's thirty-three pupils included several of Mulvany's future clients.

While James Perry undoubtedly did much to further Mulvany's career, we do not know if he employed him at his own residence, Obelisk Park, Blackrock. The present appearance of the house dates from a reconstruction (1874-75), carried out under the superintendence of the architect Sir Thomas Drew. Perry certainly employed him on two ventures at Athenry, Co Galway – the construction of a model farm on the former Oranmore estate, sold by the Incumbered Estates Court in 1850,[64] and the erection of a railway hotel (Plate 38) on the opposite side of the town. Both projects were begun in 1853 and were complete by 1854.[65] A tourist guidebook published in the latter year described the hotel, with its characteristic Mulvany bracketed eaves and a curved-roof veranda, as a 'very superior building'.

Perry was reported as having greatly developed the old estate, which was non-residential. Presumably he stayed at the hotel on his visits. The farm buildings, which flank the MGWR line, are of little architectural pretension. A Gothic steward's house (dated 1870 on a plaque) was presumably erected by the Goodbody family who inherited the property. It may well have been a late, if not particularly inspired, Mulvany design.

James Perry's brothers, William and John, owned the flour and oaten mills at Ballinagore in Co Westmeath, an extensive establishment described in 1846 as capable of manufacturing 50,000 barrels of flour and meal annually. Although William had arrived in Ballinagore in 1838 to take over the milling interests of W.H. Mulock, the Perry investment may have been made at the invitation of the proprietors of the village, the Vignoles family, kinsmen of the engineer of the D&KR. Initially the Perry brothers seem to have occupied two earlier millers' houses. William's house, single storey over basement, was extended and aggrandised in the Mulvany style before he acquired Mosstown (a manor house eight miles to the northwest) from William Dargan in 1856. Dargan had bought the Mosstown estate from the Incumbered Estates Court in 1851 (possibly as a proxy for the Perrys).[66]

John Perry, on the other hand, decided to build a large new house in Ballinagore itself (Plate 50), backing onto the flour mills but facing out into open country.[67] This was in Mulvany's picturesque style, with asymmetrical elevations and low-pitched roofs, with prominent brackets supporting the eaves and verges. It was probably begun about 1850 and was complete by 1854, when it was recorded on *Griffith's Valuation*.[68] The elaborate entrance gateway has characteristic Mulvany piers with swept caps. There is no documentary evidence that Mulvany designed the house, though it is undoubtedly his. It was mentioned in Gilbert Cockburn's obituary in *The Dublin Builder* in 1862 as having been built by his firm.[69] The same notice, incidentally, recorded Mulvany's attendance at the funeral.

Another of Mulvany's midlands clients was John Lyster of Norefields, Co Laois, who built a house with characteristic curved roofs at Bunrevan, outside Birr, Co Offaly, in 1863.[70] The estate, like others of Mulvany's *nouveau riche* patrons, had been purchased from the Encumbered Estates Court. A number of buildings in the village of Clara in the same county also bear Mulvany's imprint, though documentary evidence is lacking. What Portlaw was to the Malcomsons, Clara was to the Goodbodys, who owned the local flour and jute mills. Both towns have similar workers' housing. Mulvany probably designed the Friends' Meeting House at Clara (Plate 53), which the family built, as well as Marcus Goodbody's seat, Inchmore (Plate 54), rebuilt apparently in the 1860s. The Victorian embellishments of Charlestown (Plate 52) and Clara House, owned respectively by his brother Jonathan Goodbody and nephew Richard Goodbody, were probably also carried out to Mulvany's designs. The connection was once again through James Perry of

50 – Ballinagore, parish of Newtown, Co Westmeath (c.1850-54)
an eclectic design combining some of Mulvany's 'free-style' motifs with classical elements

51 – Cartown, parish of Kiltoghert, Co Leitrim (1856-62)
a simplified version of Ballinagore

52 – Charlestown, Clara, Co Offaly
line drawing by John Ross showing the remodelled façade attributable to Mulvany (c.1860)
(from Margaret Stewart, GOODBODYS OF CLARA 1865-1965)

53 – Former Clara Meeting House, Clara, Co Offaly (c.1860)
built adjoining the Quaker cemetery and facing the Inchmore demesne

opposite 54 – Inchmore, Clara, Co Offaly (c.1860) – portico

Obelisk Park, whose favourite daughter Hannah was married to Marcus Goodbody.

James Perry died in July 1858, two months after his business partner Joseph Malcomson. His will contained a number of contentious provisions, which probably explains why he had it drawn up by a Roman Catholic solicitor rather than another Quaker.[71] Under a codicil, the Athenry farm was left to his son William James on condition that he did not marry Elizabeth Pim of Monkstown Castle, whose late father had been employed by Perry and his associates as treasurer of the D&KR. The caveat may have been due to a business row rather than the fact that Perry's own second wife was a Pim. When the wedding went ahead, the farm passed instead to the Goodbodys, who had already got a generous slice of James Perry's estate, including most of his shares in the Hibernia and Shamrock mines. William James, who seems to have had other financial resources, threatened litigation, and eventually obtained a generous settlement from his relatives. Under its terms he handed Obelisk Park over to Marcus Goodbody in 1873.[72]

James Perry's death may also have lost Mulvany the patronage of the Midland Great Western. When they came to add a substantial colonnaded cab-shelter to the Broadstone in 1861 they employed George Wilkinson, architect to the Dublin, Wicklow and Wexford Railway. Wilkinson also got the commission for a new station building at Mullingar, to replace a temporary structure of 1848. Perry's death may also have precipitated the closure of Richard Field Mulvany's newspaper *The Advocate* at the end of 1860; the printing plant had been mortgaged to him in 1851. Richard disappears from the Dublin directories, and may have gone abroad after the collapse. Flush with funds, William James Perry left Obelisk Park for an even larger house nearby, Ardlui, which he extended and aggrandised in 1873, employing the architect John McCurdy.[73] He bankrolled his cousins' mills in Ballinagore, eventually taking over all their property there when they defaulted on repayments.[74] James Perry had arranged for his nephews John and James (whose father Robert had died in 1855) to be educated in Germany, and left them shares in the mines should they decide to work in the venture. James junior built Dean's Grange House (Plate 55) (just south of Blackrock, later renamed Clonkeen House), a villa in Mulvany's Italianate style with channelled stucco and quirky curved quoins. It was demolished in 1988.[75]

The great Malcomson house-building boom got underway in 1861, three years after Joseph's death. His estate, valued at £333,000, was one of the largest proven in Ireland in the nineteenth century. It was five times that of James Perry, who died just before him. Joseph Malcomson's brother William took over the business, though he apparently lacked the necessary acumen. Joseph's widow Charlotte withdrew her capital and left Portlaw for Bray. In 1861 she acquired Leopardstown House, Co Dublin (Plate 56), a two-storey-over-basement residence built by

55 – Dean's Grange House, Co Dublin (1863)
(incorporating parts of the earlier Grange House) demolished in 1988

56 – Leopardstown Park (formerly Leopardstown House), Co Dublin
reconstructed from Mulvany's designs, 1861-62

57 – Villa Marina, Dunmore East, Co Waterford (1861-64)
garden front

58 – Glenvar, Booterstown, Co Dublin (1855-58)
side elevation

Colonel Coote MP in the 1790s. She commissioned Mulvany to reconstruct it, inserting a top-lit imperial staircase and embellishing the façade with stucco ornaments. The work, carried out by William Crowe, was completed in October 1862 at a cost of £6,500.[76]

Joseph Malcomson's three sons each commissioned houses from Mulvany. The eldest son, David, who inherited the bulk of his father's estate, built Villa Marina (1861-64) (Plate 57) at Dunmore East, Co Waterford, employing a Dublin contractor, Mathew Lynch of Camden Street. It is the largest of Mulvany's curved-roof houses. The main block, which is symmetrical with a pair of bows facing the sea, is flanked by single storey wings as at Mayfield. There is a separate U-shaped stable block, surmounted by a cupola (now converted to a private house). Mulvany exhibited a perspective of the stables at the RHA in 1866. *The Dublin Builder* thought the style of Villa Marina 'unusual but effective'.[77] Some of the internal doors are round-headed, with hood mouldings similar to those used externally by Mulvany on other houses.

David Malcomson's brothers George and Frederick each built houses in Portlaw itself. Frederick's house, Clodiagh (Plate 59), constructed by Cockburns in 1862-63, has conventional pitched roofs, with carved and pierced bargeboards.[78] While the walls are plastered, there are distinctive tall brick chimneystacks. This is one of the few Mulvany buildings where brick of any sort can be seen. The interior is relatively simple, the main feature being a centrally located pine staircase. Mulvany exhibited a design for a conservatory and hothouses for Frederick Malcomson in 1864. These are no longer extant.

George Pim Malcomson's Portlaw House (Plate 60) (now the Woodlock convent) was begun in 1861, and is the only classical house of the three. It is a large two-storey building with a standard Mulvany single-storey D-ended wing to one side. The elevations are finished in stucco with a rusticated ground floor and shallow balconies beneath the first-floor windows. There is a fine Portland stone tetrastyle Ionic portico. George Malcomson and his wife Emilie are commemorated in a plaque over the front door. An ornate central hallway rises the full height of the house. The hall extends to one side to incorporate the staircase, as at Mount Anville. The present external appearance has been somewhat marred by the removal of the parapet and the central bow on the garden front. Another Portlaw house, Milfort, was enlarged and aggrandised by William Malcomson. Mulvany may have been involved. The house was demolished in the 1950s, as was its lodge, the curious-looking domed Copper Lodge (Plates 61, 62).

Mulvany also designed houses for two of Joseph Malcomson's brothers. Thomas built Minella (*c.*1862-64) (Plate 63) outside Clonmel, while John built Elva Lodge (1864-66) on the outskirts of Waterford city. One of the Minella lodges (Plate

59 – Clodiagh, Portlaw (1862-63)
entrance front

60 – Portlaw House, Portlaw (1861-64)
entrance front (Lawrence Collection, National Library of Ireland)

61 – Portlaw House
Copper Lodge and entrance gates, demolished in the 1950s (Lawrence Collection, NLI)

62 – Mayfield, Portlaw – wheel-operated double gates (photographed in 1982)
– the rustic fence castings are similar to those at Copper Lodge

34) is a simplified version of that at Mount Anville (Plate 33). The house itself is classical, with a pair of full-height bows on the garden elevation, which overlooks the river Suir. The main rooms are arranged around an elongated central hall which rises to roof level (similar but wider to that at Mayfield). Elva, which was later renamed Ardkeen, remained a private residence until the late 1940s, when it was acquired by Waterford County Council as the site of a sub-regional sanatorium (built 1950-54).[79] Although altered with a simplified interior and a flat roof, the house survived as part of the hospital complex until 1994 when it was torn down by the health board. Elva was not unlike Portlaw House, though its elevations were more severe. The house proper and the gate lodge (which survives) had similar tetrastyle Doric porticos.

63 – Minella, Clonmel, Co Tipperary (c.1862-64)
garden front facing the River Suir, with modern hotel additions (photo: Jacqueline Donnelly)

OTHER BUILDINGS

While most of Mulvany's practice, particularly in later years, seems to have centred on domestic commissions, he designed a wide range of other structures, from the plinth of the Thomas Moore statue in Dublin of 1857 (Plate 64),[80] to cornstores (unidentified) in Cork of 1863,[81] and the 300-bed lunatic asylum in Mullingar (1847-55) (Plates 65, 66). This was one of several asylums awarded at that time to private architects by the Board of Works, and while all were prominent in the profession, Mulvany's connection, as the brother of one of the Board's commissioners, must surely have helped.[82]

The building is unusually (for him) in the Gothic style, which was stipulated in the brief, while the plan follows the standard corridor layout advocated by the great asylum theoretician, Dr John Conolly of Hanwell, whose ideas appealed to the Board of Works. The design is competent if unexciting. No doubt if he had a choice

64 – Thomas Moore Memorial, Westmoreland Street, Dublin (1857) – plinth designed by Mulvany to support Christopher Moore's statue

Mulvany would have preferred to have used one of the other styles he favoured. Mulvany's choice of Tudor Gothic was old fashioned, and may be contrasted with the more 'progressive' Early English Gothic style of the contemporary asylums at Cork by William Atkin, and Killarney by Benjamin Woodward of Sir Thomas Deane's office, buildings which reflected the precepts of Pugin.

Mulvany served for a time as architect to the Dublin Board of Superintendence for the City Prisons, for whom he altered the Richmond Bridewell in 1850, 'augmenting the treadwheel buildings' and converting a large part of the building to the separate system.[83] This complex was subsequently rebuilt as a barracks in the 1870s, and is now Griffith College. Mulvany also carried out additions and alterations for the same board to Grangegorman Penitentiary in 1850-51.[84] However, this did not include the installation of the separate system, which had to wait until a fur-

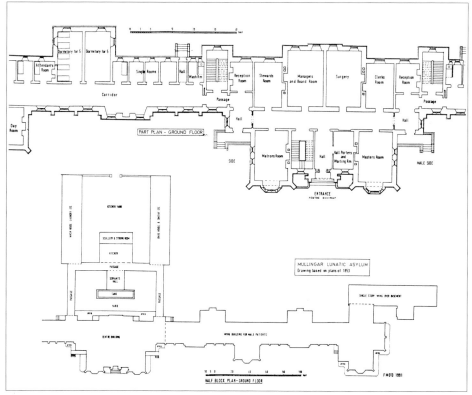

ther reconstruction, with E.H. Carson as architect, in 1865-66.

One Dublin public-building commission which might have fallen Mulvany's way had circumstances been different was the National Gallery on Merrion Square. To pay tribute to William Dargan's munificence in underwriting the Dublin Exhibition, a committee (the Dargan Committee) was set up in July 1853 to collect funds for a 'permanently useful' commemoration. Among the four trustees of the fund was James Perry. These funds were subsequently made available for the erection of a national gallery, a project which had been independently promoted by the Royal Irish Institution and which was ultimately subvented by the government.

In 1855 Mulvany's artist brother George, who was secretary of the Irish Institution, was also appointed to the board of the proposed gallery. In this capacity he somewhat bizarrely attempted to design the gallery himself, producing a series of plans and sections, which, although well wrought, displayed an ignorance of sound building construction. In 1856 Richard Griffith, chairman of the Board of Works, asked his architect Jacob Owen for a report on the designs. Owen gently suggested that George should 'abandon the office [of architect] he [had] undertaken in so liberal a spirit'. Griffith hoped to retrieve the situation by getting a professional architect to recast George's design on the quiet, suggesting that either his own staff-member Frederick Villiers Clarendon or John Skipton Mulvany 'might agree to take on the job at little, or, possibly, no cost'.[85] In the event, the task was entrusted to Owen's son-in-law, the successful architect and surveyor Charles Lanyon. Ultimately, even he was superseded, the final designer being Captain Francis Fowke RE. George Mulvany survived the debacle to be appointed director of the gallery in 1862.

While Mulvany was associated with the new rich of the 1850s – the wealthy middle class who purchased bankrupt estates in the aftermath of the famine – he did receive some commissions from the Ascendancy. In 1862 he exhibited at the RHA a 'south-west view of proposed alterations to Dunbrody House, Co Wexford, the seat of Rt. Hon. Lord Templemore'. The extent of his work there is unclear; some, if not most, of his additions appear to have been swept away when the house was again remodelled about 1900. Templemore's cousin, the Marquess of Donegall, was commodore of the Royal Irish Yacht Club.

Mulvany's name has also been associated with buildings on the estates of another aristocratic family, the Crichtons (Earls of Erne) of Crom Castle, Co

---

Mullingar District Asylum (now St Loman's Hospital) (1847-55)

65 – Entrance front (photo: D. Newman Johnson)

66 – Part-plan of ground floor (top) and half-block plan (bottom)
(drawings by the author, 1991, based on original tracings now in the National Archives)

Fermanagh. It has been suggested that he designed the Gothic revival parish church at Crom (1840-44).[86] The Butter Market at nearby Lisnaskea was erected from his plans in 1856. This is also Gothic, and has been described as a hybrid of medieval German and Tudor revival styles.[87] Mulvany had some connections with the area. The Lisnaskea Market House proper was designed by his master William Deane Butler during the period of his apprenticeship. William Mulvany's in-laws, the Winslows, were prominent landowners in nearby Kinawley.

Another Ascendancy family for whom Mulvany appears to have worked were the Garnetts of Williamstown, Co Meath. A dower house on the estate, Williamstown Lodge, probably built about the time of the proprietor's marriage in 1859, has a typical curved roof. Another attributable houses include Gigginstown, Co Westmeath (Plate 67), a formal classical building erected about 1853-55 for Elizabeth Busby of Churchtown House, Co Dublin, and Cartown (originally Summerhill), near Carrick-on-Shannon, Co Leitrim, and the enlargement of Belmont, Cullahill, Co Laois. Gigginstown superseded an earlier house in the demesne, which Miss Busby inherited from Captain Brabazon Connor in 1853. It is more Georgian than Victorian, with decorative plasterwork, small-paned windows and a tetrastyle Doric portico.[88] The rooms are laid out symmetrically, with a characteristic Mulvany top-lit imperial staircase. The grand entrance gates and lodge are also attributable to him (Plate 68).

Cartown (Plate 51), an unpretentious gabled villa with round-cornered windows at ground-floor level, was built for George Church on the site of a small farmhouse on a ninety-three-acre holding. It was described in *Griffith's Valuation* in 1856 as vacant and 'unfinished', but was completed by 1862.[89] Belmont, otherwise Aghnacourt, is a Georgian house, the seat of John Roe in 1837, which was sold by members of the Ponsonby family to Robert Owen in 1861.[90] It was presumably at this time that a single-storey cottage orné extension with a typical Mulvany curved roof was built at right angles to the original block to face the entrance avenue.

Aside from the attribution of Crom Church, only two ecclesiastical projects by Mulvany are known – an unexecuted design for remodelling the Mariner's Church in Kingstown, exhibited at the RHA in 1863,[91] and a convent in St John's, Newfoundland, completed about 1850.[92]

LIFE AND DEATH

Little is known of Mulvany's private life, but he never remarried. According to Professor Butler, he was fond of the Ascendancy sport of foxhunting, an interest he shared with his brother William.[93] Butler (citing the late-Victorian architect Albert

Gigginstown, parish of Killulagh, Co Westmeath

67 – Entrance front (c.1853-55)

68 – Gates and lodge

(photos: Irish Architectural Archive)

E. Murray) claimed that he was also a 'prodigious smoker of cigars'. We know, though not from Murray, that Mulvany's elegant lifestyle was also the cause of a deteriorating liver condition. This lifestyle was in marked contrast to the austerity of most of his Quaker patrons, though he did have a soulmate in Marcus Goodbody of Clara, a keen huntsman who both smoked and drank.[94]

In 1854 Mulvany was elected a member of the Royal Irish Yacht Club, whose building he had designed seven years earlier. He was proposed by Joseph Todhunter, a Quaker and kinsman of the club secretary. He was one of the first architects to join the Kingstown yacht clubs. Membership did not, of course, imply an active interest in sailing. During his sixteen years as a member of the club, Mulvany sponsored only one candidate for membership himself. That was his client, George Pim Malcomson of Portlaw. Joseph Todhunter seconded the proposal. In 1863 Mulvany was elected a director of the Dublin and Kingstown Steam Packet Company, a short-lived company which provided a steamer service between the two ports.[95]

Whether Mulvany sailed or not, he was involved in one celebrated maritime incident which nearly cost him his life. During a gale on Saturday 9 February 1861, two colliers were driven on to the rock armouring at the back of Kingstown's East Pier. The commander of the guardship *Ajax*, Captain Boyd, and five of his men perished while trying to rescue the crew of one of the foundering vessels, the *Neptune*. A number of bystanders assembled on the pier were swept against the rocks, some with serious injury. Mulvany, who had perhaps sauntered down from the Royal Irish, where a ship wrecked the previous day was lying against the foreshore, was among the group, but remarkably he emerged unscathed.[96] He survived another nine years to die of cirrhosis in May 1870 at the age of fifty-seven.[97] There is a certain poignancy in his death certificate. His martial status, recorded as bachelor, is corrected to read widower.

He left effects valued at under £1,000. There is no evidence that his practice was sold or taken over or that any of its records (which must have been considerable) were preserved. In November 1870 the annual report of council of the Royal Institute of the Architects of Ireland recorded that Mulvany had 'at one time been one of the most extensively employed practitioners in Ireland'.[98] Someone must have commissioned a bust by Thomas Kirk Stewart, which was exhibited in Dublin in 1871 and 1872,[99] but it too is untraced.

———

ACKNOWLEDGEMENTS

My initial researches into the career of John Skipton Mulvany arose from a request to lead a walking tour of the Dún Laoghaire yacht clubs in 1982, which was later developed into a lecture and eventually led to an article on Mulvany, commissioned by John Stafford, which appeared in *Martello* in 1988. My thanks to the owners of Mulvany buildings and all those who assisted me in my research over the years, in particular Daniel Gillman, the late Robert Jacob, Rob Goodbody, David Griffin, Ann Martha Rowan, Majella Walsh, Peter Pearson, Jeremy Williams, Stephen Daly, Michael Killeen, James Martin, the late Jeanne Sheehy and Kevin Murray. Among the holders of archives, I wish to thank particularly the Irish Architectural Archive, the Irish Railway Record Society, the Library of the Religious Society of Friends and the Royal Irish Yacht Club.

ILLUSTRATIONS

All photographs by the author unless otherwise stated.

ENDNOTES

1   M. Craig, *Dublin 1660-1860* (London 1952) 305.
2   A.E. Richardson, *Monumental Classic Architecture in Great Britain and Ireland during the Eighteenth and Nineteenth Centuries* (London 1914) 87-88.
3   R.M. Butler, 'J.S. Mulvanny [sic] RHA: the story of an eminent Irish architect', in *The Irish Builder*, 28 June 1924, 569-70.
4   The paper is expanded from research originally commenced for a lecture delivered to the Old Dublin Society on 16 March 1983, an illustrated synopsis of which was published in *Martello* (summer 1988) 30-41.
5   K. Bloemers, *William Thomas Mulvany (1806-1885): Ein Beitrag zur Geschichte der rheinisch-wesfalischen Grossindustrie und der deutsch-englischen Wirtschaftsbeziehungen im 19. Jahrhundert* (Essen 1922).
6   A.C. Mulvany, *Letters from Professor Thomas J. Mulvany RHA to his eldest son William T. Mulvany Esqre, Royal Commissioner of Public Works Ireland from 1825-1845* (1907) preface.
7   Walter G. Strickland, *A Dictionary of Irish Artists*, 2 vols (Dublin and London 1913) ii, 156.
8   J.C.I. Dooge, 'William T. Mulvany (1806-1885)', abstract of the Nicholas Callan Memorial Lecture delivered to the Institution of Engineers of Ireland, 22 October 1996.
9   T.J. Mulvany (ed.), *The Life of James Gandon...* (Dublin 1846) 199.
10   Mulvany, *Letters from Professor Thomas J. Mulvany*, 27.
11   See RHA catalogues and A.M. Stewart, *Royal Hibernian Academy of Arts: Index of Exhibitors, 1826-1979*, 3 vols (Dublin 1986-87).
12   Ex info. K.A. Murray and John Burnett.
13   Mulvany, *Letters from Professor Thomas J. Mulvany*.
14   Jeanne Sheehy, 'Railway Architecture – its Heyday', *Journal of the Irish Railway Record Society*, vol. 12, no. 68 (October 1975) 125.
15   Drawings in the Murray Collection, deposited in the Irish Architectural Archive, 92/46/823-35. The terrace was designed for Thomas Gresham by George Papworth in 1832 but was altered and completed from the designs of William Murray in 1833-35.

[16] For the D&KR, see K. A. Murray, *Ireland's First Railway* (Dublin 1981).

[17] F. O'Dwyer, *Lost Dublin* (Dublin 1981) 129. Date on the balusters in the neo-Grec stair tower. The Ionic colonnade across the façade recalled Mulvany's yacht club designs.

[18] Joseph Lee, 'Merchants and Enterprise: the case of the early Irish railway 1830-1855', in P. Butel and L.M. Cullen (eds), *Negoce et Industrie en France et en Irlande aux XVIIIe et XIXe Siecles* (Paris 1980) 153.

[19] O'Dwyer, *Lost Dublin*, 126.

[20] Among the most interesting is the house illustrated here (no. 2) – a double-fronted house with a Tower of the Winds portico – which was damaged by fire in December 1999.

[21] Peter Pearson, *Between the Mountains and the Sea: Dun Laoghaire-Rathdown County* (Dublin 1998) 192.

[22] Murray, *Ireland's First Railway*, 22.

[23] Pim's 'seat' was part of a composition exhibited by Papworth a the RHA in 1829. This would indicate that the house, Carrickbrennan Lodge, was designed by Papworth rather than Mulvany, as suggested by Pearson, *Between the Mountains and the Sea*, 185.

[24] N. Niven, *A prospectus of the proposed pubic gardens at Monkstown Castle, Dublin* (Dublin 1839).

[25] Some of the Crofton Road houses are fronted by railings with 'capstan' balusters similar to those at Mulvany's Royal Irish Yacht Club.

[26] Registry of Deeds, Dublin, 1858/19/155.

[27] Mount Jerome Records.

[28] Mount Jerome Records; *Daily Express*, 5 July 1852.

[29] Registry of Deeds, Dublin, 1857/22/90.

[30] Murray, *Ireland's First Railway*, 167-71.

[31] The iron roof was removed in the 1960s. The main station platform has been altered several times, most notably for the DART (1983) and for a disabled access bridge (1997) which has bisected Mulvany's buildings.

[32] For these aqueducts, see Ruth Delany, *Ireland's Royal Canal 1789-1992* (Dublin 1992) 65, and Michael Barry, *Across Deep Waters: Bridges of Ireland* (Dublin 1985).

[33] A number of Mulvany and Papworth drawings for the clubhouse, formerly in the collection of the Office of Public Works, are now in the National Archives, Dublin.

[34] Minute books of the Royal Irish Yacht Club.

[35] *The Builder*, 10 August 1850, 375. A ground plan published in *The Builder* in 1851 (148) is reproduced (redrawn) in Maurice Craig, *The Architecture of Ireland from the earliest times to 1880* (London and Dublin 1982) 299, fig. 254.

[36] Peter Pearson, *Dun Laoghaire Kingstown* (Dublin 1981) 39.

[37] Jeanne Sheehy, *Kingsbridge Station* (Ballycotton 1973) 7.

[38] Sheehy, 'Railway Architecture – Its Heyday', 137.

[39] Michael Killeen, 'Broadstone – Railway Station to Bus Garage', *Dublin Historical Record*, xxxiv, 4 (Sept 1981) 141.

[40] Craig, *Dublin 1660-1860*, 300.

[41] A wash drawing of the Westport gateway displayed in the house is ascribed to James Wyatt with a date of 1805, but as the plate in Papworth's book purports to be of a speculative design for 'an unostentatious entrance to a small property of the superior class', I consider that the Westport design must postdate it. Papworth is known to have been working for the proprietor,

Lord Sligo, in London in the 1820s and designed an ice house for Westport in 1831. I thank David Griffin for bringing *Rural Residences* to my attention.

[42] The station closed to passenger traffic in the late 1980s when the old GSWR station on the Westmeath side of the town was reopened.

[43] The principal alterations to the hotel have been the erection of superstructures on the roof in the 1960s and the replacement of the original timber sashes with aluminium windows in the mid-1980s. The sash windows of the station house were replaced with top-hung PVC windows at about the same time.

[44] *The Builder*, 22 October 1853, 654.

[45] The gateway, which originally stood alongside the lodge at the Goatstown end of Mount Anville Road, was moved to its present location beside the main house during the course of road widening in the 1960s.

[46] Jeanne Sheehy, 'John B. Macneill', *Irish Georgian Society Bulletin*, xvii, nos 1-2 (Jan-Jun 1974) 22-24.

[47] Claremont was sold to a firm of developers in 1998 who lodged a planning application in 1999 for its demolition and replacement by a block of apartments. A further application was under appeal at the time of writing.

[48] Bonnie Flanagan, *Stately Homes around Stillorgan* (Dublin 1991) 62.

[49] Described and illustrated in J. Nolan, *Changing Faces* (Dublin 1982) 210, pl. 46.

[50] Before its completion it was sold twice: to William Hamilton in 1857, and in the following year to its first resident, the Quaker soap manufacturer John Barrington.

[51] *The Irish Builder*, 15 May 1870, 114.

[52] *The Dublin Builder*, 1 November 1862, 278.

[53] Described in *The Dublin Builder*, 1 May 1859, 54. In more recent times the house had an association with the architect Raymond McGrath, whose painting of it is illustrated in Donal O'Donovan's *God's Architect* (Bray 1995) 216.

[54] The façade of Merrion Hall survives as part of the Davenport Hotel, while Wesley College was demolished in the early 1970s; see O'Dwyer, *Lost Dublin*, 47.

[55] *The Dublin Builder*, 15 July 1862, 175.

[56] The Malcomsons' enterprises have been the subject of many studies, including, most recently, two essays in *Decies: Journal of the Waterford Archaeological & Historical Society*, 53 (1997): Tom Hunt, 'The origin and development of the Portlaw cotton industry, 1825-1840', 17-32, and Bill English, 'Waterford Steamship Company', 67-89; see also Desmond O'Neill's booklet, *Portlaw: A nineteenth century Quaker enterprise based on a model village*, published by the Historical Committee of the Religious Society of Friends in Ireland in 1992; and Hunt's *Portlaw, County Waterford 1825-1876 – Portrait of an Industrial Village and its Cotton Industry* (Dublin 2000). A major unpublished account is Margaret T. Fogarty's MSc thesis 'The Malcomsons and the economic development of the Lower Suir Valley 1782-1877', NUI (UCC) 1968. The genealogical information on the Malcomsons and the other Quaker industrialists is derived from a number of sources, including the National Archives, the Webb family trees in the Religious Society of Friends' Library in Dublin, and the late Robert Jacob.

[57] For a history of the mine, one of the enterprises from which the modern VEBA conglomerate emerged, see Heiner Radzio, *Unternehmen mit Energie: Aus der Geschichte der Veba* (Dusseldorf 1990). I am grateful to Stephen Daly for bringing this book to my attention.

[58] J.D. Forbes, *Victorian Architect: the Life and Work of William Tinsley* (Bloomington, Indiana

1953) 60.

[59] The building is illustrated in Michael Ahern, 'The Quaker Schools of Clonmel', *Tipperary Historical Journal, 1991*, 128-32. I am grateful to David Butler for this reference.

[60] I am grateful to Majella Walsh who has unravelled the architectural evolution of Mayfield from valuation maps and other records. See Walsh, 'Portlaw: A model industrial village', *MUBC 1995*, NUI (UCD). Although the Malcomsons went bankrupt in 1877, the Portlaw mill continued to operate (latterly as a tannery) until 1987. In recent years, Mayfield, which had been in office usage since 1955, has fallen on hard times. Although listed by the local authority, it was partly dismantled in 1987 when interior fittings were sold off, and has since been severely vandalised. It was offered for sale in 1999, but the situation was unchanged at the time of writing (*Irish Times*, 20 September 2000).

[61] T.G. Kiely, 'Notes on the construction of the old cotton factory at Portlaw', typescript (n.d., 1960s). Kiely specifically cites the school and hall as having been designed by Mulvany, which suggests that he had seen the original drawings.

[62] William Malcomson's business interests in Limerick included the railway, the Annacotty Peat Works and the Lax Weir Fisheries at Corbally, the latter being purchased in 1857. It may be a coincidence that Parteenalax, a substantial residence on the other (Clare) bank of the river, has a fabric-covered curved roof. According to Hugh Weir's *Houses of Clare* (Whitegate 1986), Parteenalax was completed by R.D. O'Brien in 1901.

[63] Michael Quane, 'Quaker Schools in Dublin', in *Journal of the Royal Society of Antiquaries of Ireland*, 94 (1964) 47-68.

[64] Registry of Deeds, Dublin, 1854/17/134.

[65] *The Builder*, 1 January 1853, 8; 30 July 1853, 484. The farm is now part of an agricultural college, with further buildings added from the designs of William A. Scott in the early 1900s.

[66] Registry of Deeds, Dublin, 1856/34/142.

[67] National Archives, Dublin, 997/778/1-11. These papers include deeds, wills and maps pertaining to the Perry holdings in Ballinagore. While the erection of the house by John Perry is referred to, there are no plans among the documents nor any reference to Mulvany.

[68] Most of the windows had small Georgian-type panes, but the larger sheet-glass panes in the reception rooms indicates a post-1845 date. Most of the windows on the principal floors were replaced by PVC units by a previous owner in the 1980s. The internal ornament is restrained, though there is a typical Mulvany overdoor in the hall as well as some characteristic plasterwork.

[69] *The Dublin Builder*, 15 February 1862, 43.

[70] *The Dublin Builder*, 15 January 1863, 10. The builder was John Dwyer of Dublin.

[71] National Archives, Dublin, probate T 12740.

[72] Ex info. Rob Goodbody, whose history of Obelisk Park was published in the *Proceedings of the Blackrock Society*, 7 (1999), 24-33.

[73] Drawings in the Irish Architectural Archive, McCurdy & Mitchell Collection. See also Pearson, *Between the Mountains and the Sea*, 236-37.

[74] The mills encountered financial difficulty in 1861 (Valuation Office, Dublin), but it was not until after William Perry of Ballinagore died in 1874 that William James put the squeeze on William's nephews Henry and Robert, sons of John (builder of Ballinagore House), who had died in 1864.

[75] Pearson, *Between the Mountains and the Sea*, 151-2.

[76] Irish Architectural Archive, PKS Collection, 77/1/L1 and 77/1/A3.

[77] *The Dublin Builder*, 15 May 1861, 508. See also the issue of 15 April 1864, 70.

[78] Irish Architectural Archive, PKS Collection, 77/1/B02/15, priced bill of measurement for extra works, June 1863.

[79] Frederick O'Dwyer, *Irish Hospital Architecture: A Pictorial History* (Dublin 1997) 26, 86.

[80] *The Builder*, 18 July 1857, 410. This was a competition-winning design.

[81] *The Dubin Builder*, 15 January 1863, 10.

[82] O'Dwyer, *Irish Hospital Architecture*, 10-12.

[83] *The Builder*, 3 August 1850, 368.

[84] *The Builder*, 3, 31 August 1850, 368, 416; 9, 16 August 1851, 517.

[85] Catherine de Courcy, *The Foundation of the National Gallery of Ireland* (Dublin 1985) 34.

[86] Alastair Rowan, *The Buildings of North West Ulster* (Harmondsworth, 1979) 223.

[87] Charles Brett, *Court Houses and Market Houses of the Province of Ulster* (Belfast 1973) 82-83.

[88] The valuation house book for Killulagh Parish (National Archives, Dublin) states in 1853 that the house was 'under construction but nearing completion'.

[89] Valuations of 1856, 1860 and 1862: Griffith's Valuation and valuation book for 1860-1904, Carrick-on-Shannon electoral district, parish of Kiltoghert, Valuation Office, Dublin. Cartown is now a hotel and nightclub. The original sash windows have been replaced with PVC units.

[90] Registry of Deeds, Dublin, 1861/12/53/294. Owen is recorded as the owner of 360 acres at Belmont in 1876. I thank Jeremy Williams for drawing Belmont to my attention. He has also suggested that Mulvany had a hand in the remodelling of Tourmakeady (originally Tarmacady) Lodge, Co Mayo, for a daughter or niece of the proprietor, the Hon Robert Plunket, Dean of Tuam (1802-67). The work was reputedly paid for by their kinsman the Hon William Conyngham Plunket, Archbishop of Dublin (1828-1897). The summer lodge, which stood on a 1,700-acre estate on the shores of Lough Mask, developed around a *cottage orné* core.

[91] *The Dublin Builder*, 15 June 1863, 101. The church was subsequently remodelled in 1865-66 to a design by Thomas Turner.

[92] *The Builder*, 31 August 1850, 416, reported that Dr Fleming, bishop of Newfoundland had bequeathed £300 towards completion of the building.

[93] Butler, 'J.S. Mulvanny [sic] RHA: the story of an eminent Irish architect'.

[94] Margaret Stewart, *Goodbodys of Clara 1865-1965* (Clara 1965) 16.

[95] *The Dublin Builder*, 15 January 1863, 9.

[96] *The Irish Times, Daily Express*, 11 February 1861. I am grateful to Dónal Ó Suílleabháin, author of *O Kingstown go Dún Laoghaire* (Dublin 1976) for this reference. See also John de Courcy Ireland, *Wreck and Rescue on the East Coast of Ireland* (Dublin 1983) 67-72.

[97] According to the probate grant in the National Archives, he died in a house on Clonliffe Terrace, Dublin (no house number given) where he had moved from Trafalgar Terrace. This may have been the address of someone who was nursing him.

[98] *The Irish Builder*, 1 December 1870, 285.

[99] Strickland, *A Dictionary of Irish Artists*, ii, 402-3. The bust was exhibited at the RHA in 1871 and at the Dublin Exhibition of 1872.

The Medlycott Farm, Roundwood, Co Wicklow
the farm's cattle-run is hidden behind these borders

The traditional Irish farmhouse and cottage garden

PATRICK BOWE

THE HISTORY OF IRISH GARDENING, AS IT HAS BEEN WRITTEN TO DATE, HAS TENDed to be the history of the gardens of the aristocracy and the gentry. Much documentation, both written and pictorial, survives about these gardens. However, there is a parallel history – that of the farmhouse and cottage garden of which fewer records remain. It is more difficult, therefore, to conjure up a picture of their design and planting. Research on this subject has also been impeded by the erroneous assumption that there has been no tradition of cottage gardening in Ireland in the same way that such a tradition existed in England. However, a little investigation reveals the case to be otherwise.[1]

It is true, for example, that in many western areas where living was at subsistence level, the cultivation around a cottage was often restricted to a small enclosed potato patch. However, prosperous farmers and cottagers, particularly in areas of the country where the soil is more fertile, boasted gardens which were a traditional mixture of flowers, fruit and vegetables.[2] Most of these have now been abandoned, or swept away in modernisation schemes. However, careful observation while travelling around the country will still reveal an occasional traditional garden of this type, often being cared for by an owner of an older generation. One wonders how long many of these gardens will last. It is an apt time to initiate a record of their character and purpose.

Nineteenth-century books and journals provide scattered references to Irish farmhouse and cottage gardens. The writings of Mary Leadbeater and Martin Doyle are particularly rich in information. Mary Leadbeater was born a member of the Quaker family of Shackleton living at Ballitore, Co Kildare. Between 1811 and 1822, she wrote a series of pamphlets on the economy of the cottage and its garden, which were intended to be read by cottagers.[3] Some of the pamphlets took the form of short biographies of cottagers she had known. Others were in the form of dialogues between fictional cottagers but based on her knowledge and observation of the behaviour and language of the cottagers she encountered around Ballitore. The purpose of the pamphlets was to impart, in an interesting and entertaining manner, hints as to how life in a cottage and its garden might be improved. One of the pamphlets, for example, includes a basic garden calendar with details of simple garden tasks to be performed month by month.

Her pamphlets were followed between 1828 and 1868 by the books of Martin Doyle, the nom de plume of the Rev William Hickey, a clergyman from Ballyorley, Co Wexford (Plate 1). His books were published in a compact format to make them widely affordable. Two comprehensive handbooks, *Practical Gardening* (1833) and *A Cyclopaedia of Practical Husbandry* (1839) were the best known.[4] Throughout his life, he contributed articles to jour-

1 – Martin Doyle, author of A Cyclopaedia of Practical Husbandry, *published in Dublin in 1839 (NLI)*

nals on the subject of farming and gardening on a small holding, and between 1833 and 1840 was co-editor (with Edmund Murphy, a landscape gardener) of *The Irish Farmers and Gardeners Magazine*.[5] By 1852, interest in the subject of cottage gardening in Ireland was such that the *The Cottage Gardener*, a London journal, thought it worthwhile advertising itself in the journal of the Royal Agricultural Society of Ireland, and arranging for McGlashan, the Dublin bookseller, to stock copies.[6]

Cottage gardening was encouraged through the awarding of annual prizes for well-kept gardens by local farming societies such as the Navan Farming Society,[7] the North Wexford Agricultural Society and the South Wexford Agricultural Society (founded *c.*1818), to name but a few.[8] Philanthropic societies were also encouraging. The Irish Peasantry Society of London offered for some years an amount of £15 for the encouragement of neat cottage dwellings and gardens within the area of the

Wexford Poor Law Union.[9] In 1837, the Agricultural Society of Ireland offered a prize for an essay on cottage gardening.[10]

Individuals were also convinced of the need to support the development of cottage gardening. In 1838, Ninian Niven, the director of the Botanic Gardens at Glasnevin, Dublin, proposed to build some model cottages within the garden. They were to be lived in by staff members, who would cultivate small gardens around them for the instruction of the visiting public.[11] An improving landlord, Hamilton Knox Grogan Morgan of Johnstown Castle, Co Wexford, reserved one of the cottages on his estate for occupation by an horticultural instructor, who, by teaching and example, would encourage the other cottagers to maximise the use of their plots.[12] The improvement of flower, fruit and vegetable types was encouraged by the distribution, often free of charge, of surplus seeds and seedlings from the garden of the nearby mansion house.

By gleaning a variety of contemporary publications, it is possible to build up a composite picture of the typical Irish farmhouse and cottage garden of the period with respect to its size, design, planting and maintenance. Before examining these details, it may be useful to quote two word-pictures of a typical garden's overall aspect. Martin Doyle described a prize-winning garden:

> The garden before the house was small but well cropped, fruit trees growing in the borders, and the young thorn quicks which had been planted in the breast of the surrounding fence, carefully preserved from weeds; carrots, parsnips, turnips, cabbages, onions and beans thriving well, and in a sheltered corner there stood nine or ten bee-hives ... A few hop plants and roses appeared over the front wall, nor were these plants unprofitable: Mick had sold the hops on the preceding year for five shillings, and the roses were taken by the neighbouring apothecary in exchange for some medicines...[13]

Mrs Leadbeater described a cottage garden near Arderin c.1780:

> The cottage ... had its walls half-concealed with ivy; woodbine in luxuriant clusters, hung from the roof; the little garden behind was fenced with a thick hedge of whitethorns, intermingled with dog roses; and the summer house, impervious to the rays of the sun, was formed by two shady trees of alder...[14]

CONTEXT AND SIZE

The size of small holdings varied. In towns, weavers and labourers might have but a simple cabbage patch, usually big enough to grow about a hundred plants. In the country, an acre of potatoes, considered enough to feed a family of six for a year, together with another acre for pasturing a cow, was considered the minimum. However, in areas of poorer soil, the holdings were larger.

Arthur Young, the English agriculturalist, whose *A Tour in Ireland* was published in 1775, writes that cabins in Co Cork usually had four to five acres.[15] He later relates that cabins at Woodlawn in Co Galway had eight or nine acres, two or three cows or two cows and a horse, two or three pigs, many poultry, a rood of flax (for manufacture of the cottager's linen) and a half acre of potatoes.[16] Elsewhere, smallholdings had some sheep, the wool from which provided the raw material for the family's clothing.

The rear of the house was the location of a small farmyard, which included a dung hill that was very important for the manuring the garden. The garden, also varied in size, was located in a separately enclosed area next to the farmhouse or cottage. In some places it lay between the house and the public road; in others it lay also along the public road but to one side of the cottage. In Curracloe, Co Wexford, the location of each garden with respect to its cottage varies along the length of the village street (Plate 2). A more formal grouping is seen in the architectural drawings published by Martin Doyle in *A Cyclopaedia of Practical Husbandry* for a combined group of four cottages and their gardens (Plate 3).[17]

2 – Curracloe, Co Wexford, photographed by Kevin Danaher in 1947;
the informal village-scape shows the differing relationship between the cottages and their gardens
(Dept of Folklore, University College Dublin)

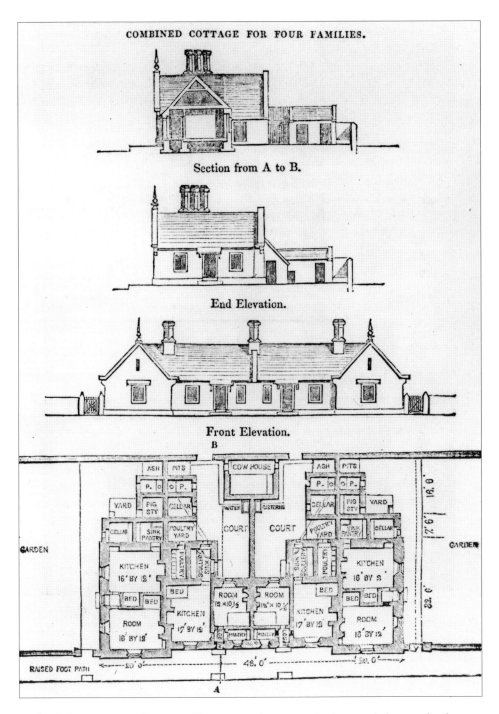

3 – A CYCLOPAEDIA OF PRACTICAL HUSBANDRY – the entry under 'cottages' shows a plan for a combined cottage for four families with its associated farm buildings and gardens (NLI)

ENCLOSURE

The garden area was walled or hedged to restrict the entry of farm animals, but also to provide shelter for the garden's small plants. Walling, being permanent, was preferred in areas where field stone was available.[18] However, hedging was a more widely used form of enclosure. Sometimes a hedge was grown not from the ground, but along the top of a grass bank.

The most widely used plant material for hedging was hawthorn or whitethorn, sometimes planted in a double row. Both plants being thorny, they grew into a stock-proof hedge if well maintained. A mixture of whitethorn and the thorny sweet-briar rose, known as eglantine, was also recommended.[19] As the whitethorn flowered in spring and the pink-blossomed eglantine in summer, the hedge was decorative in two seasons of the year. The native dog rose (*Rosa canina*) was also used in the same way. Mixed hedges, containing evergreens such as common holly,[20] and common laurel,[21] were also popular, as these evergreens helped provide good winter shelter. The sally willow, or sallow, was recommended as a hedging plant because its flexible young shoots might be used as the raw material for baskets, which most cottages knew how to make.[22] The osier, a related willow with narrower leaves, was also recommended. In some exposed locations, a cottage might be entirely surrounded by sheltering willow.[23]

Later in the nineteenth century, Monterey cypress, introduced from California, and fuchsia, introduced from South America, were commonly used for hedging, the latter in milder areas only.[24] Occasionally, a taller tree was incorporated in a hedge to provide extra, high-level shelter. For this purpose, elm was sometimes used but ash was preferred since the wood from its shorter branches was useful in the home manufacture of domestic and farm implements.[25]

GATES

The gate in a boundary hedge was usually of the picket type, constructed of wood and hung on wooden posts. It was usually black-tarred to ensure its long-term preservation. Although black might seem, at first glance, a somewhat funereal choice, the cottage windows and door were also traditionally tarred, and both stood out in crisp contrast against the white limewashed colour of the cottage walls. If the cottager could pay, a wooden gate might be replaced by an iron one of local forge manufacture. Iron gates were painted with lead oxide preservative paint, as were the corrugated iron roofs which replaced thatch on some cottages in the late nineteenth century. In counties like Kerry and Wexford, the lead oxide paint was treated as an undercoat and given a scarlet finishing coat, scarlet being the complementary colour of the prevailing green of the Irish countryside.

Frequently, the boundary hedge was trained over the gate to form an imposing entrance arch.[26] Less frequently, the garden gate was flanked by a pair of sentinel Irish yews.

PATHS

A garden in front of a farmhouse or cottage was usually divided by a narrow path leading from the gate to the front door. The path surface might be constructed of simple compacted earth, needing careful sweeping to keep it tidy. More expensive to make and maintain was a gravel path. The path edging was often made with a line of limewashed field stones. However, dwarf box-hedging, sometimes cut casually with a scythe rather than a fine shears, was also effective as an edging.[27] A row of strawberries as a productive substitute for box was occasionally recommended. A second path around the perimeter of the garden was maintained so the housewife could bring the family's washing to dry on the garden's boundary hedge.

BOWERS

Mrs Leadbeater describes the use of summer houses or shady bowers, formed by training and pruning the flexible branches of willow trees. One of the male characters in her *Cottage dialogues* asserts of his garden: 'I am going to plant sallows there to make a little summer house for my mother to sit in while she watches her bees.' Mrs Leadbeater also describes how a bower was a treasured place for a housewife to sit knitting with her family at the end of a summer's day. Sweet peas and sweet-smelling woodbines were sometimes grown up through the willows' branches so that the bower might be suffused with their scent.

WALL BORDERS

Borders directly under the front wall were a feature of many farmhouse and cottage gardens. In the case of cottages built directly along the roadside, the wall border may have been the only space available in which to garden (Plate 4). The soil was often retained by a line of whitewashed stones (Plate 5). Perennial flowers, shrubs and climbing plants were grown in informal mixed groupings (Plate 6). Wall shrubs

4 – A cottage at the Strawberry Beds, Dublin, is adorned with skilful roadside planting

5 – Scalp Cottage, The Scalp, Co Dublin
with its traditional white-washed field stones used as edgings to beds and borders
(illustrations courtesy National Photographic Archive, Lawrence Collection)

6 – A thatched house and garden, probably in the west of Ireland, showing the mixed planting of climbers, shrubs and perennials in the wall border – note the rainbow (Dept of Folklore, UCD)

7 – The fantastical and whimsical topiary of a cottage at Headfort, Co Meath
(National Library of Ireland)

were topiarised to prevent them from becoming too large and shading the already small windows. Topiary is a feature of Irish cottage gardens, as it is of small gardens throughout Europe – it being necessary to confine trees or shrubs which outgrow the modest space available for them. Sometimes topiaries were allowed to develop into fantastically whimsical forms (Plate 7).

GENERAL PLANTING

The interior of the garden was developed with a mixed planting of fruits, vegetables and flowers grown together in a more or less formal arrangement of large beds, the beds often edged with dwarf box hedges. In their formal pattern, they can be said to be imitative on a smaller and simpler scale of the larger ornamental gardens of the aristocratic mansion. In fact, Martin Lacy describes the farmhouses on the Johnstown Castle estate as having parterres in front of them. Some of the farmhouses at Ballykilcavan, Co Laois, and at Doneraile, Co Cork, still maintain formal box beds in front of them (Plate 10). The traditional pattern of box-edged beds surviving in the garden of 78 Upper Leeson Street, Dublin, although located in a city garden,

8 – Killala Cottage, Newmarket-on-Fergus, Co Clare
showing the use of exotic plants such as New Zealand flax with its sheaves of sword-like leaves
(Dept of Folklore, University College Dublin)

serves to indicate to us such a box-hedged arrangement and mixed planting (Plate 9). Martin Doyle recommends hedges of rosemary instead of box. However, no other account of its use as a hedging material in a small garden of the period has been found.[28]

At the beginning of the twentieth century, many gardens began to display spiky plants with architectural foliage, such as New Zealand Flax or Cordyline Palm, both natives of New Zealand (Plate 8). Their sheaves of sword-like leaves strike an exotic note in the Irish countryside.

WALL PLANTS

Samuel Hayes of Avondale, Co Wicklow, in his book *A Practical Treatise on Planting* (1794), noted in the village of Abbeyleix 'the comfortable, and at the same time, picturesque cottages, with their accompaniment of eglantine and honeysuckle in their little paled-in gardens'.[29] Mrs S.C. Hall in her account of a journey through Ireland – *Ireland, its Scenery, Character, etc.* (1841-43) – also wrote of cottages, this time in Piltown, Co Kilkenny, 'each adorned with climbing roses and honey-suckles'.[30] Many such accounts refer to honeysuckle and climbing roses growing on a farmhouse or cottage wall. The honeysuckle variety seems to have been the native honeysuckle (*Lonicera periclymenum*), known colloquially as woodbine. The climbing rose varieties recorded are more various. The eglantine referred to above is the pink-flowered native rose, *Rosa eglanteria*. However, a red-flowered climbing rose was also grown. This appears to have been the Apothecary's Rose (*Rosa gallica* 'Officinalis'), since its leaves were used by apothecaries in making healing infu-sions of many kinds, as indicated in Martin Doyle's description of a cottage garden referred to above. Cottagers also used the leaves in homemade teas for the treatment of sore throats, and in concocting ointments for treating skin abrasions.

One account refers to quite a different rose on a cottage wall: 'the yellow rose'. Although its exact or botanical name has not been traced, it may have been the French tea-noisette, R. 'Desprez a Fleur Jaune'.[31] The most popular cottage roses during the twentieth century were the summer-flowering rambler roses such as R. 'Dorothy Perkins' and R. 'American Pillar', with abundant bright pink small flow-ers in large clusters.[32] Today, old French roses like R. 'Bourbon Queen' and R. 'Felicite et Perpetuee' are frequently seen growing on the wall of a large farmhouse.

On some cottage walls, fruit trees such as apples and hops were trained, espalier frames being constructed of slender ash poles.[33] One source recommended cottagers to grow whitecurrants as wall plants because they could be sold profitably for the making of the then popular whitecurrant wine.[34]

FLOWERS

Flowers were useful in a small garden because their nectar was collected by the cottager's bees. Flowers, when cut, were also used in decking the altar of the local church, a household shrine or a corpse when it was being waked. Mary Leadbeater mentions that cultivated flowers were also useful in fashioning a presentation posy when the landlord or his wife came to visit.[35] Mignonette, old-fashioned primroses in different coloured seedlings (Plate 11), and sunflowers are some of the flowers mentioned in descriptions. For example, Mary Leadbeater recounts the use of the latter in a farmhouse garden: 'a garden of four acres contained one or more bowers, cherry trees, and a sundial beside which, as in rivalry, rose stately sunflowers'.[36]

Bright tropical flower colour was added to the nineteenth-century cottage garden by the cultivation of pot-grown pelargoniums (often known erroneously as geraniums). These were usually lined out on window cills in summer; in winter they were transferred to the inside cills. In milder areas of the country, pelargoniums were planted in a wall border, and would survive winter after winter outside, often growing into tall woody shrubs dramatically displaying their bright red flowers for many months of the year.

HERBS

Farmhouse and cottage gardens contained herbs, the dried leaves of which were used for brewing medicinal teas and also in concocting cures for the ailments of farm animals.[37] The dried leaves of sage, marigold, camomile, rhubarb and fennel were popular for these purposes, as were sprigs of rosemary.[38] Parsley, thyme and savory were grown in more sophisticated gardens for use in flavouring cooked vegetables and meats.

VEGETABLES

Mary Leadbeater's book *Cottage dialogues among the Irish Peasantry* illustrates a cottage gardener's annual vegetable growing routine:

> I set out early York cabbage plants far enough apart to plant a bean between. At the edges of my early potato ridges, I plant green borecole. When the potatoes are dug, the borecole grows large and gives fine greens for the winter. The later potatoes may have later borecole plants, or single grey peas put

at the edges and by this way the ground is made most of. Besides this you see, I love my little plants of beans and pease [sic], my beds of turnips, carrots, parsnips and onions: the trimmings of these, and of the cabbage, are thrown to the pig. After the season is over, I plant rape seed, enough for 500-1,000 plants. They stand over the winter, when all else is fallow and I feed the shoots to the cow and the pig.[39]

The principal vegetable crop was potatoes. Hely Dutton noticed about twenty-five varieties, some of them familiar to us today, being grown in Co Galway in 1824: Grenadiers, Red apple, White apple, black, Early Prussians, Cups, Lumpers, English Reds, Cork reds, Barbers wonders, Bangors, Red nose kidney, Leather coats, White eyes, Windleers, Pink eyes, Ox noble, Yams or bucks, Coppers, Purple kidney, American dandies.[40] However, a wide variety of green vegetables was also grown. The agriculturalist, William Blacker of Castle Blacker, Co Armagh, was precise in his recommendation of the quantity and type of vegetables a small farmer ought to sow each year:

Common Peas, Marrow Peas and Beans – 1 pint of seed

Carrots, Onions and Parsnips – 1 ounce of seed

Leeks, Common Cabbage, Savoy Cabbage, Broccoli
and Cauliflower – $1/2$ ounce of seed.[41]

This may seem a plentiful variety of green vegetables. However, in many cottage gardens the variety being grown was considerably less. In his survey of Co Clare published in 1808, Hely Dutton noted that 'Almost every cottier has a small garden chiefly occupied with cabbages: some few sow onions, parsnips etc.' [42] In other early nineteenth-century descriptions, turnips, lettuce, celery, 'common grey peas' and 'small horse beans' are mentioned. French beans were grown on tall, freestanding frames in some gardens, but they were considered, on the whole, a vegetable for the 'quality', that is, people who lived in grander houses.[43] In the smallest gardens, only flat Dutch cabbage was grown in addition to potatoes.[44] (Cabbage grown next to seaside cottages and fertilised with seaweed was considered particularly delicious at that time.)[45]

A neatness of appearance in the vegetable garden was encouraged by William Doyle. He recommended that peas and beans should not be allowed to run to seed after cropping, but should be cut down to within three inches of the ground to present a tidy aspect. Such pruning was also recommended because it might result in an additional crop in October.[46] Another late-season ornament of the vegetable garden must have been the thatched dry-earth mounds which were constructed over the cabbages to preserve them after cropping.[47] Mrs Leadbeater writes of a woman, Betty Bryan, who made cabbage nets for sale. Nets such as these, neatly set over the plants to protect them from foraging birds, must have added to a cared-for appearance of a vegetable plot.[48]

BUSH FRUIT

Blackcurrants and gooseberries were the most commonly grown of the bush fruits.[49] They were grown in lines between rows of vegetables and flowers. Although it was intended their bulk would give wind shelter to young seedling vegetables and flowers, their location was carefully chosen so as not to shade the smaller plants in the garden. Farmers or cottagers who had an orchard often preferred to grow them in one of the orchard's corners.

ORCHARDS

In very small gardens, a fruit tree was incorporated among the vegetables and flowers. In gardens of greater extent, fruit trees were grown in a separate enclosure or orchard (Plate 12). A small orchard typically consisted of between ten and twenty trees, mostly apples grafted on crab apple stock. Common varieties of apple grown in Co Meath, according to R. Thompson in his 1802 survey of that county, were 'summer crofts, winter crofts, jenetings, the eve, Ross nonpareil or French pippin, the golden pippin, the Harvey and the London tankard'.[50] A much greater variety was grown in Co Armagh, famous then, as it is today, as an apple-growing county. Larger farm orchards also had pears and, occasionally, cider apples.[51] For many centuries the cider apples of the Blackwater valley in Co Waterford were renowned, as were the cherries of the area.[52] In some old cottage orchards today, the grass under the trees is carpeted with snowdrops and daffodils, and the perimeter grass banks are covered by montbretia.

BEES

Martin Doyle recommended that 'no smallholder should be without bees'.[53] They were usually kept in straw hives raised on wooden stands and located within the shelter of one of the garden's hedges.[54] Bees not only produced honey but also wax, which was sold for making candles, among other things. The bees would collect nectar from the flowers of beans, buck wheat, thyme, borage, sage and mustard which were grown in the garden for that purpose. Fruit trees, when in blossom, also provided nectar, as did wild furze, broom, clover and heather in the countryside nearby.[55] Excellent honey was produced in cottage gardens which were located near a hill or bog abundant in heather.

MAINTENANCE

The cottage garden was owner-maintained. The larger farmhouse garden was also owner-maintained, but the services of a paid 'weeder-woman' were sometimes employed.[56] The hoe was a common implement. A light spade for digging, a rake and a pitchfork were also useful tools. A small iron-plough, drawn by a cow or horse, was used for cultivating the ground for larger vegetable sowings.[57] Hedges were clipped with shears, although Mary Leadbeater describes how at one cottage scissors were used: 'They keep the hedges well trimmed, and when disappointed of the garden shears which a neighbour used to lend them, Bridget used her scissors for the purpose.'[58]

Children were sometimes employed in clearing stones and hand-weeding. In Mary Leadbeater's *Cottage dialogues*, a fanciful picture of the part played by children is conjured. A cottage woman asserts: 'My little boys nail sticks together to give them a pretty shape and the girls put down French beans about them, and they run up among the sticks and blossom and look a pretty picture.'

Vegetable surplus such as potato stalks, bean stalks and spent cabbage leaves was useful in feeding the farmyard pig or cow. What they would not eat was mixed with weeds pulled from the garden and fallen autumn leaves in season to provide the pig's litter. In turn, the cleanings from the pigsty and the cow shed were added to the dung-hill, the manure from which, when well-rotted, was used to fertilise the garden. So, there was a close interdependence between farmyard and garden.

THE TRADITION TODAY

The revival of interest in the traditional Irish arts and crafts at the beginning of the twentieth century was paralleled by a revival of interest in traditional Irish farmhouse and cottage gardens (Plates 13-17). Articles in books such as *Irish Rural Life and Industry* (1906), and in periodicals such as *The Irish Homestead* (1895-1923) and *Irish Gardening* (1906-16) encouraged the interest. During the 1920s, a member of the culturally influential Purser family, Mrs Nuttall, created a still-maintained garden near Roundwood in Co Wicklow in this vernacular style (Plates 18-21).

The contemporary failure to recognise the existence of an Irish farmhouse and cottage gardening tradition has led to the unwitting destruction over a long period of time of this part of Ireland's garden heritage. The purpose of this article is to encourage the recovery of interest in this tradition so that the few gardens which remain in each area might be conserved or, at least, recorded. The tradition might then inform the design and planting of our smaller gardens in the future, and so ensure the continuity of this aspect of our garden history.

———

ACKNOWLEDGEMENTS

Nicola Gordon Bowe, Trevor Elkinson, Frances-Jane French, Criostoir MacCarthaigh, John and Elinor Medlycott, Department of Irish Folklore at University College, Dublin, National Library of Ireland, National Photographic Archive, George Thomas, Joan Williams.

ILLUSTRATIONS

Photographs by the author unless otherwise stated.

ENDNOTES

[1] Other Irish gardening traditions which remain to be investigated if a comprehensive history of Irish gardening is to be realised include that of the rectory and presbytery garden, that of the city and town garden, and that of the planting of public malls and parks.

[2] Such were the gardens of the tenants of Hamilton Knox Grogan Morgan of Johnstown Castle, Co Wexford. In praise of this gentleman, Thomas Lacy wrote in his book *Home Sketches* (1852) 276: 'The comfortable and substantially built and slated farm-house, with its neat garden or orchard, and its tasteful parterre, will speak, in language not to be misunderstood, his best eulogium ... while his day-labourers dwell in neatly-slated cottages, where the creeping woodbine, or mayhap the sweetly scented rose, declares, in silent but convincing terms, that comfort and comparative refinement are not strangers to those who live within the range of his influence and bounty.'

[3] *Cottage dialogues among the Irish Peasantry* (Dublin 1811), *The Landlord's Friend* (Dublin 1913) and *Cottage biographies* (Dublin 1822).

[4] Others were *Hints originally intended for the small farmers of Co Wexford* (1828) and *Notes and Gleanings related to the County of Wexford* (Dublin 1868).

[5] See, for example, Martin Doyle, 'Gardens for the Labouring Classes', *Irish Penny Journal*, Saturday 26 September 1840, 111.

[6] *Royal Agricultural Society of Ireland and Irish Agriculturalist*, June 1852, 29.

[7] R. Thompson, *A Statistical Survey of Co Meath* (Dublin 1802) 334.

[8] Martin Doyle, *Notes and Gleaning relating to the County of Wexford* (Dublin 1868) 109.

[9] *ibid.*

[10] *Irish Farmers and Gardeners Magazine*, iv (Dublin 1837) 150. In the same article, cabbages, lettuces, onions, potatoes, beans, celery, parsnips, carrots, turnips and leaks are recommended for cottage gardens, as are strawberries planted as an edging along the garden walks. Gooseberry quicks in lines to divide up the garden and shelter the vegetable rows are also suggested.

[11] E.C. Nelson and E.M. McCracken, *The Brightest Jewel, A History of the National Botanic Gardens, Glasnevin, Dublin* (Kilkenny 1987) 86.

[12] Doyle, 'Gardens for the Labouring Classes', 93.

[13] Martin Doyle, *Irish cottagers* (Dublin 1833) 6.

[14] Mary Leadbeater, *Cottage biographies*, 84. The dog rose (*Rosa canina*), with its pink to white flowers, is a native Irish plant and can still be seen growing spontaneously in many country hedgerows.

[15] Arthur Young, *A Tour in Ireland...* (London 1775) 277.

[16] Nelson and McCracken, *The Brightest Jewel*, 246.

[17] Martin Doyle, *A Cyclopaedia of Practical Husbandry* (Dublin 1839) 113.

[18] The clearing of field stones from agricultural land made the land easier to plough as well as providing raw material for walling

[19] *Rosa eglanteria*, preferring lime soils, was not suitable for growing on Ireland's many acid soils.

[20] Samuel Hayes, *A Practical Treatise on Planting* (Dublin 1794). He recommends planting hollies every four feet in a mixed hedge.

[21] Doyle, *Hints originally intended for the small farmers of Co Wexford* (1828) 19.

[22] Hely Dutton, *A Statistical Survey of Co Clare* (Dublin 1808) 145. The sally (*Salix caprea*), being bushy rather than tree-like in growth, is ideal for hedging. The osier (*Salix viminalis*), another bushy willow was also used. The Red Huntingdon willow, also known as the timber sallow, was a willow variety recommended by Martin Doyle in his *Cyclopaedia of Practical Husbandry*, 324.

[23] Nelson and McCracken, *The Brightest Jewel*, 341. Isaac Weld in his *Survey of the County of Roscommon* (Dublin 1832) 256, also describes a little garden surrounded by willows.

[24] Edward Malins and Patrick Bowe, *Irish Gardens and Demesnes from 1830* (London 1980) 112. The fuchsia is *Fuchsia magellanica*.

[25] Nelson and McCracken, *The Brightest Jewel*, 86: 'slender ash poles are valuable for hoops, spade and pitchfork handles, rakes, tails and garden espaliers: if a little grosser, and somewhat crooked they make the best plow handles, horse hames and swingle trees...'

[26] Doyle, 'Gardens for the Labouring Classes', 94: 'Opposite the house is the garden, entered by an arch cut in a high alder hedge, which has an imposing appearance.'

[27] Martin Doyle, *Practical Gardening* (Dublin 1833) 38.

[28] Doyle, *Cyclopaedia of Practical Husbandry*, 74

[29] Nelson and McCracken, *The Brightest Jewel*, 154.

[30] Mrs S.C. Hall, *Ireland: its Scenery, Character, etc*, 2 vols (London 1841-43) ii, 62.

[31] It was raised in France in 1830.

[32] These hybrid ramblers were raised in the United States in the first decade of the twentieth century, and soon established themselves in popularity throughout the temperate world

[33] Hayes, *A Practical Treatise on Planting*, 86.

[34] Leadbeater, *Cottage dialogues*, 79.

[35] Doyle, 'Gardens for the Labouring Classes', 83.

[36] *Irish Farmers and Gardeners Magazine*, iv (Dublin 1837) 143.

[37] See the copy of *Kidder's Receipt Book* which belonged to the Borbridge family of Inch, Co Wexford, in which concoctions for the treatment of sick or injured animals are inscribed in manuscript. I am grateful to Mrs John Medlycott for showing me this.

[38] Oliver Goldsmith, *The Deserted Village*, 7th ed (London 1772) 13.

[39] Doyle, 'Gardens for the Labouring Classes', 88. 'Borecole' is what we call 'kale' today.

[40] Hely Dutton, *A Statistical Survey of Co Galway* (Dublin 1824) 353.

[41] William Blacker, *An Essay on the Improvement to be made in the cultivation of small farms* (Dublin 1845) 54.

[42] Doyle, *Practical Gardening*, 177

[43] Doyle, 'Gardens for the Labouring Classes', *Irish Penny Journal*, 26 September 1840, 87.

[44] Hall, *Ireland: its Scenery, Character, etc*, 353

[45] *ibid.*, 202

[46] Doyle, *Cyclopaedia of Practical Husbandry*, 33

[47] *ibid.*, 57.

[48] *Irish Farmers and Gardeners Magazine*, iv (Dublin 1837) 27.

[49] Dubourdieu, *A Statistical Survey of Co Antrim* (Dublin 1812) 438, notes the increasing variety of gooseberries available in Co Antrim.

[50] *Royal Agricultural Society of Ireland and Irish Agriculturalist*, 1852, 236

[51] V. Sampson, *A Statistical Survey of Co Londonderry* (Dublin 1802) 438, observes that 'farm houses usually have orchards with apples as well as pears'. Samuel Hayes in his *Practical Treatise on Planting*, 33, refers to the famous cider apples which grew on the banks of the Blackwater in Co Waterford. He also cites the celebrated Irish cider apple variety known as Cacagee.

[52] The variety known as the Affane cherry is mentioned, for example, in Charles Smith, *The ancient and present State of the County of Waterford* (Dublin 1746) 78

[53] Doyle, *Cyclopaedia of Practical Husbandry*, 103

[54] Doyle, 'Gardens for the Labouring Classes', 334.

[55] Doyle, *Cyclopaedia of Practical Husbandry*, 103.

[56] Doyle, 'Gardens for the Labouring Classes', 178: 'Timothy dresses gardens...' is the only reference I have found to a man whose profession it was to journey around putting gardens into shape in the same way that a landscape gardener might do today.

[57] Hall, *Ireland: its Scenery, Character, etc*, 163.

[58] *ibid.*, 94.

————

9 – The French garden, Upper Leeson Street, Dublin.
The rare survival of a traditional Dublin city garden illustrates the use of box-edged beds of mixed plantings, which was also characteristic of the small rural garden.

10 – A box parterre, with beds in which flowers, vegetables and fruit trees grow, at Doneraile, Co Cork

11 – Old-fashioned primroses of mixed colours fill box-edged beds at Maidenhall, Co Kilkenny

opposite

12 – The apple orchard, underplanted with daffodils, of the Thomas cottage at Greenane, near Rathdrum, Co Wicklow

The Thomas Cottage, Greenane, Co Wicklow

13 – The walled and hedged garden in front of the cottage

14 – Garden walls of field granite are topped with decorative quartz stones. On the left of the handmade gate are hung lucky horseshoes.

opposite

15 – Box-hedges with rounded contours line the path to the rose-framed door

16 – The view from the cottage door down the garden path

17 – Flowering rhododendrons and columbines are followed in summer by flowering martagon lilies, bistorts and montbretias

*The Medlycott Farm, Roundwood,
Co Wicklow*

*18 – The farm's cattle-run is hidden behind
these borders*

*19 – Mixed borders of cottage flowers
encroach on the narrow garden path*

opposite

*20 – Box-edged vegetable beds intermingle
with the flower beds*

*21 – Traditional yew topiary flanks the gate to
the farmyard*

St Lasarian's, Leighlin
View of the cathedral from Grose's ANTIQUITIES OF IRELAND

The large medieval churches of the dioceses of Leighlin, Ferns and Ossory: a study of adaptation and change – part II

ANA DOLAN

THE FIRST PART OF THIS STUDY EXAMINED THE MAIN AGENTS OF CHANGE THAT affected the medieval churches, and was published in this author's article in the second volume of *Irish Architectural and Decorative Studies* (later referred to as *IADS*, ii). This second part examines the individual histories of the twelve churches investigated, and the range of conservation issues presented by them.

The founding of the churches during the Anglo-Norman invasion was described in the previous article, as was the difference between a monastic church and a parish church. The two major changes of the sixteenth century, the Suppression of the monasteries and the Reformation, and their impact on the church buildings were also examined. Throughout the seventeenth century, as political and religious fortunes fluctuated, so too did the ownership of the churches. Repossessions by one side or another of the religious divide were common, bringing further changes to the church building. During the eighteenth century, despite the prosperity of the country, the condition of the churches declined sharply, with many completely ruined. The activities of the Board of First Fruits between the years 1777 and 1823 resulted in an impressive church-building programme. The reforms of the nineteenth century were the result of many years' agitation by the emerging Catholic community.

The first six case studies are the great medieval churches of the Anglo-Norman towns. The final six are monastic foundations: three Augustinian, two Cistercian and one Dominican. In each study the location, history and subsequent development is described, with particular emphasis on changes to the building fabric. The intention is to identify common threads that run through the histories rather than provide detailed architectural description or analysis of the age or condition of the various parts of the structure.

It should be noted that the plans of the churches are published in the second volume of this journal (*IADS*, ii, pl. 6, 36-37). The later modifications also are shown in the same volume (pl. 12, 56-57). They are reproduced at the end of this article for convenience.

ST MARY'S, CALLAN

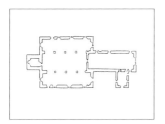

Callan is located fifteen miles south-west of Kilkenny, on a bridging point of the King's river, which is a tributary of the Nore. The town was relatively large and probably enclosed by a ditch. St Mary's parish church is prominently located in the centre of the town, beside the market place, at the junction of the main street and the road from the bridge. There was an Augustinian abbey located just outside the town walls, which is now a national monument in State care. William Marshall is generally credited with founding the town of Callan and also with building the church *c*.1220. The church prospered, and by the year 1300 St Mary's had annexed the tithes of the parishes of Tullamaine, Cooliaghmore, Killaloe, Ballycallan and Tullaroan.

The west tower is the oldest surviving part of the building and dates from the thirteenth century. During the fifteenth century all the original church was taken down except for the square tower or presbytery at the west end, and what is now know as the ancient parish church of Callan was erected on its site.[1] The fifteenth-century church consisted of a long rectangular chancel and a nave with wide aisles. There is a chapel on the south side of the chancel and traces of another chapel on the north side. The square tower of the first church has been incorporated into the later church as a west tower. The fifteenth-century church may be built on the site of the earlier one in order to retain the relationship of the church and tower. There is a modern wall separating the nave and chancel. The ruins are largely intact, with eight complete arches to the nave aisles and a large number of traceried windows and richly decorated doorways. Leask included sketches of the doors in his book on Irish churches. Externally, there is a bold batter to the base of the walls which finishes at a stringcourse. The nave and its relatively wide (3.8m / 15 feet) aisles had separate span roofs, the stone gutter for which was carried along the tops of the arcade walls. To allow for a sufficient slope or fall westward in the gutters above, the arches are kept low and the effect is rather clumsy.[2] The chancel is 18m long and

6.1m wide internally; the south wall of the chancel is 1.45m thick. The ancient baptismal font, with plain fluting on the four sides, and of huge proportions, stands immediately inside the entrance door.[3]

In 1641, during the Confederation of Kilkenny, the church returned to Roman Catholic hands, with Sir Nicholas Shee, who called himself 'Parson of Callan by jurisdiction from Rome', as rector.[4] In 1647 he was succeeded by Bartholomew Archer, another Roman Catholic, but by 1660 a Protestant minister is again rector. In 1731, Bishop Otway reported that 'Callan church, next to St Canice's, the largest in the diocese; west end needs repairing.'[5] These repairs were not carried out, for the following year, the chaplain, Vere-Hunt, was admonished to repair the north and south chapels. In 1781 the parish union included Callan, Tullaroan, Tullowmain, Coolaghmore, Killaloe and Ballycallen, with two churches in repair. In 1795 the church was in repair again, but by 1799 the nave of the church is 'now a ruin, but the chancel is kept in repair and used as the parish church'.[6]

In Robertson's *Antiquities of County Kilkenny* there is an illustration of the church *c*.1813 (Plate 1). The view of the church is from the north-east, and the chancel is shown as a roofless ruin with ivy growing over the walls. There is a finial shown on the apex of the east gable which is now missing. The doorway on the north wall of the chancel once led into a partially demolished structure on the north side of the chancel. The side chapel on the south side of the chancel is also ruined and roofless. The west tower appears to be in good condition, with battlements and a roof.

Callan Union was a wealthy parish, with an annual income in 1833 of £2,415, all of which belonged to the incumbent. The Board of First Fruits did not grant either a loan or a gift to the church, but in 1837 their successors, the Ecclesiastical Commissioners, granted £393 for the restoration of the chancel. The work consisted in re-roofing the existing chancel and side chapel for use as a church. The restoration was carried out with little regard for the fabric of the earlier church, as shown in a photograph of the junction of the east gable of the south aisle with the new roof (Plate 2). The masonry of the east gable of the south aisle is hacked away where the new roof of the chancel is carried across it.

In 1949 the Commissioners of Public Works were appointed guardians of the ruins of the nave, the north and south aisles and the western tower by the Representative Church Body. The church in the chancel was in good condition in 1952 and was in use for worship (Plate 3). Conservation work was carried out on the west tower and the south aisle between 1949 and 1952 by the National Monuments department of the Office of Public Works. The ground levels inside the nave which had built up as a result of burials were also reduced at this time. In 1959, Percy le Clerc, Inspector of National Monuments, noticed that the south arcade had sunk since works were last carried out. There was a gap of three inches

St Mary's, Callan

1 – William Robertson's illustration showing the church in ruins c.1813

2 – A photograph from the National Monuments file showing the east gable of the south aisle where it was hacked away in 1837 to accommodate the new roof

opposite

3 – The church in repair in 1952

4 – The conservation work in 1959. The south arcade is ready to be taken down.

Callan . S. Mary's . X. 1952

between the flaunching on the top of the wall of the arcade and the wall itself. The arcade was about nine inches below its proper level. The subsidence was most likely due to the use of the nave as a burial place. The arcade was carefully recorded and taken down. A new concrete foundation was laid, and the arcade was rebuilt on top. Approval was given for an expenditure of £2,500, but the actual cost was £2,480![7] Photographs from the National Monument's photographic library document this extensive restoration work (Plate 4).

By 1974 the roofed portion of the church was closed for public worship and was subjected to frequent vandalism. The Representative Church Body approached the National Monuments service and requested that the rest of the building also be taken into State care. Louis Feeley, Clerk of Works, inspected the church and reported that it was in 'excellent condition. The roof was particularly attractive and had best quality slating ... there was woodworm in most of the church furniture ... set in the floor are several fifteenth century grave slabs, ornately cut and in a remarkable state of preservation.'[8] The transfer was finally completed in 1976, and the entire building became a national monument. The contents of the church were stripped out by the RCB before handing it over.

The church building at Callan is the latest in date of the case studies. It has survived virtually intact, with minor modification carried out in 1837. These changes were hardly respectful of the medieval fabric, but no major demolition was undertaken. The Board of First Fruits was not involved with this church. Some of the restraint shown may have been due to the increase in interest in Gothic architecture, but it is more likely due to the modesty of the loan from the Ecclesiastical Commissioners. The roofed chancel is currently in poor condition, with no daylight as the windows are boarded up to protect them from vandalism. There is no electric light in the church so it is difficult to view the interior (*IADS*, ii, pls. 11, 55).

ST MARY'S, GOWRAN

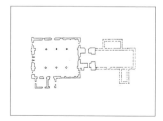

Gowran is located in the eastern edge of the fertile Kilkenny lowlands on a small tributary of the Barrow river. After the Norman invasion, Gowran was granted to Theobald fitz Walter, Chief Butler of Ireland and ancestor of the Ormond family. Before his death in 1206, he granted a charter of incorporation to his free burgesses of 'Ballingaveran'. He is also thought to have appropriated the rectory or moiety of Gowran to the Knights Templars, who are found in possession as early as 1254.[9] The town of Gowran was partly walled, with trenches and ramparts making up the rest of the enclosure.[10] The church is located on the southern side of the town within the enclosure, set slightly back from the main street.

When the Knights Templars were suppressed, the church was passed to the Knights Hospitallers.[11] The church at Gowran, which was a secular college with four priests or vicars, continued to enjoy the patronage of the Butler family. In 1321 Edmond le Botiller, Earl of Carrick, who died in London, was brought back to Gowran and buried. In 1337 his son James, 1st Earl of Ormond was also buried here. The 3rd Earl, also James, was buried in Gowran in 1404, although he had acquired Kilkenny castle in 1391. The manor of Gowran remained in the possession of the Ormond family until *c*.1700, but by that time the family lived elsewhere.

In the Royal Visitation Book of 1615, four priests are mentioned living together as a group in their college. Gowran was captured by Cromwell in 1650 after a short siege. Bishop Tennison reported in 1731: 'the chancel is well paved and even. All between the belfry and west end of the church are in ruins, a nave and two aisles. One bell in the steeple. An English school and a Latin school under different masters. Minister's house no better than a cabin.' [12] In 1795 the rector reported the 'church in repair', but this probably refers to the chancel only. In 1799 £2 was spent on repairs of the church.

The church consists of a chancel with a tower between it and the double-aisled nave. Gowran is best known for the quality and richness of the stone carving, described by Roger Stalley as the work of the 'Gowran Master'. In 1793 Grose included an illustration of the church, as well as a plan, in his *Antiquities of Ireland* (Plate 5). It is fortunate that we have a plan of the building which predates both the collapse of the north aisle arcade and the restoration work of the next century, which included the demolition of the chancel. In Grose's plan, the chancel arches on which the tower is carried are shown open. There are three triple windows on the south wall of the chancel, as well as a large window in the east wall. There are side chapels to the north and south of the chancel. Both the north and south nave arcades are shown. The north aisle is subdivided into four small recesses, while the south aisle has three recesses with two further side chapels beyond. Grose's illustration of the church from the south-east shows the chancel roofed with a stepped east gable wall (Plate 6). The three sets of triple windows are shown in the south wall, as well as the smaller structure which is a ruin. The nave of the church has two aisle arcades to full height, although the entire structure is roofless and covered with ivy. The tower is also covered in ivy and there is an indication of a roof over the tower.

In the *Fourth Report of the Ecclesiastical Commissioners (Ireland)* of 1833, Gowran was described as 'a church capable of accommodating 150 persons, built in 1827 by means of a loan of £738 granted by the late Board of First Fruits'. In

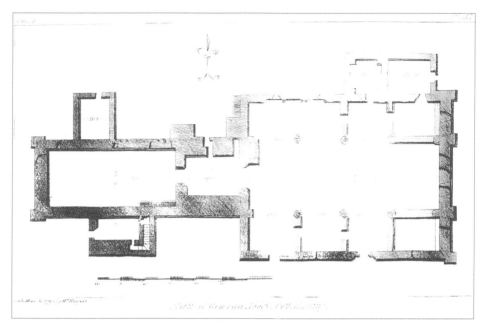

St Mary's, Gowran

*5 – Grose's plan of 1791 showing the chancel before it was demolished
and the south aisle arcade before it fell*

6 – Grose's view of the church showing the chancel before it was demolished

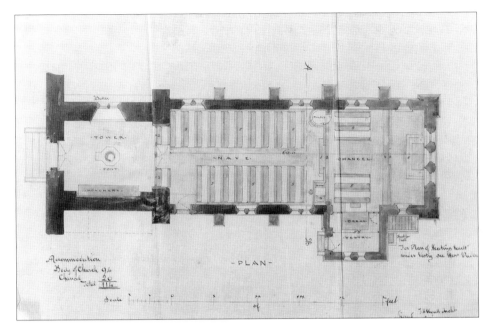

St Mary's, Gowran

7 – T.H. Wyatt's proposals for the restoration of the church at Gowran c.1872
– plan of tower and church

8 – Wyatt's proposed sections and east elevation

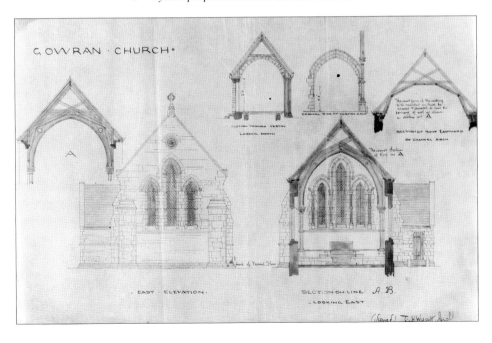

Lewis' *Topographical Dictionary* the church is described as

> restored in 1826 ... The ruins very interesting details in the early English style among which are a finely pointed arch of black marble leading into the chancel: a series of similar arches supported by circular and octagonal columns; some windows of elegant design, delicately ornamented in quatrefoil and several interior chapels: the doorways and baptismal font are black marble curiously sculpted.

William Robertson, author of the *Antiquities of County Kilkenny,* was most likely the architect for the works undertaken at Gowran in 1827. A drawing signed by William Robertson, but not dated, is in the National Monument's archive, and most likely represents this restoration (*IADS*, ii, pl. 13, 58). The works to the church involved demolishing the chancel and building a new church on its site. The plan is of the entire building, including the earlier part which is referred to as 'the Ruin'. There are also two cross-sections through the new building: the longer section is through the new church and the tower and the short section is across the new church. The drawing is beautifully executed and coloured, and shows details of the interiors. The vaulted arch underneath the tower mentioned by Lewis is not shown. The south arcade is shown to have a different plan shape than the north arcade. During the course of the current works, the cement render was removed from the interior of the church, and evidence was found of earlier openings in the south wall, which correspond to those in Robertson's drawing.

Following the Disestablishment of the Church of Ireland in 1870, the RCB received compensation and began a programme of church-building. Thirty-five years after the new church was built on the site of the chancel it was almost entirely rebuilt. In 1872 the prominent English architect Thomas Henry Wyatt was employed to carry out the work, which was an attempt to adapt the existing simple 'prayer book church' to the ideas of the Gothic Revival. The church as it exists today differs slightly to Wyatt's plan and sections, which are in the RCB library (Plates 7, 8). The plan shows the altar in the 'chancel' raised above the 'nave'. A series of altar rails separate the nave and chancel. There is an attempt to introduce a 'choir' with the seats facing each other, and the organ is in the vestry. The pulpit and desk are shown at the 'chancel arch'. The box pews are replaced by rows of seats all facing towards the altar. The external walls have new buttresses attached, which are modelled on the buttresses in the original church. They appear to be an intrinsic part of the structure, but in reality are decorative. The sections show an elaborate chancel arch supported on circular columns which were not built (Plate 8).

At the time, there was some public debate about the restoration. *The Irish Builder* of January 1872 reports that 'some rebuilding and alterations are proceeding at the parish church of Gowran according to the designs of Mr. Wyatt, Architect, of London.' The article goes on the quote *The Kilkenny Moderator*, in which there were 'objections to certain parts of the work' and 'some of the alterations made by the architect are in very questionable taste'. The *Moderator* continues as follows;

> ... the entrance to the church (as now being rebuilt), Mr. Wyatt's original plan was that it should be through the ruins of the ancient nave, the door being placed where it had been before the rebuilding of the choir, early in the present century, in the lower story of the belfry tower. But interments have since taken place very quickly in the old nave, so that any path through the ruins must of necessity pass over several graves. To avoid this, Mr. Wyatt arranged that a door should be made from the exterior in to the tower in a place where the wall is already arched for the purpose of admitting a loop hole or small light' so that the entrance to the re-edified church, in place of being connected with a passage through the ruins of the nave, will be in close proximity to the place in which the former chief entrance to the choir was, but passing in through the tower. We can only say that we regret very much that the original features of the original tower are to be at all interfered with, even so far, and we do hope that if a door way is there made, care will be taken that it shall be in as close keeping as possible with the original details. Great caution seems to us to be necessary in meddling with the tower in any way, for one of the piers on which it is supported seems in a very shaky state. We are very sorry to perceive that it was deemed necessary to remove altogether the lower vaulting of the tower, apparently with the view of giving the same elevation as the choir roof to the portion of the belfry which will form part of the church. However, that which most offended our eye, in a late inspection of the building, was the apparent intention of permitting the south door of the recent church still to continue in its original design of 'church warden gothic'. There are some other matters in connection alluded to by our contemporary which it seem to think will mar the entire design of restoration.

Although the *Moderator* regretted the destruction of the vaulting underneath the tower and the insertion of the new doorway, the principal objection was to the particular style of 'church warden Gothic' as adopted by Wyatt.

Even as late as 1872 the destruction of medieval structures was viewed as lamentable but not entirely unacceptable. Despite the superficiality of Wyatt's version of Gothic and the misgivings of the *Moderator*, there was a definite attempt to integrate the newer building with the original church. The window and door details of Wyatt's church are faithful, yet strangely dull copies of the original stone carvings. The windows of the new church are based on the original but without the carved heads (Plate 9). The omission of the carved stops and their substitution with a plain square box may be an attempt at distinguishing the new from the old. If this is the case, it marks an advance in the way additions to existing structures were carried out. However, the destruction of the vaulting underneath the tower indicates a lack of sensitivity to the original stone carvings.

As in Callan, the older part of the church, including the upper two storeys of the tower, were first passed into the care of the National Monuments service. The new church continued in use until about 1970, when it became redundant. The church remained empty for a number of years until it too was transferred into State care. The Representative Church Body stripped the church of its furniture and fittings before it was handed over. The medieval font and the bust of Charles Agar were moved to St Laserian's in Co Carlow. When the modern church was transferred into State care, the roof was in very poor condition due to water penetration. In 1996 the entire roof was stripped and all decayed timber was removed and replaced. The roof was felted and battened and re-slated using the original slates and ridge tiles. The church is currently being restored by Dúchas, the Heritage Service, and will be open to the public in 2001. The fine medieval carved box tombs and carved effigies will be displayed in the modern church.

9 – St Mary's, Gowran
the original thirteenth-century window (left) and the T.H. Wyatt's copy c.1872 (right)

ST MARY'S, KILKENNY

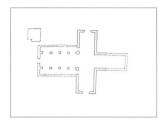

The church of St Mary's is located in the centre of Kilkenny city, just off High Street, behind the Tholsel. The church lies in the heart of the medieval town, surrounded by a network of narrow, stepped laneways. According to Bishop Rothe, the original church of St Mary's was founded merely as an oratory, in which the inhabitants of the southern division of the town might assist at Mass without having to make the journey to St Canice's cathedral for that purpose.[13] The Church of Blessed Mary was a William Marshall foundation, built between 1202 and 1218, and it served as the parish church for the Hightown of Kilkenny. The present church is cruciform in shape and was originally aisled. The nave, transepts and part of the chancel all date from the thirteenth century. A bell tower was added in 1343.[14] Rocque's map of Kilkenny from 1757 shows a freestanding tower to the north-west of the church (Plate 10).

St Mary's was considered the church of the merchant classes, and the Corporation kept the church in repair and also held their meetings in the choir and in the bell-tower before the Reformation. In 1333, the Corporation of Kilkenny ordered that a chaplain should be paid to celebrate mass in St Mary's. There is an account in the records of Kilkenny Corporation of miracle plays being acted out in the church in the sixteenth century.[15] Before the Reformation, one half of the rectory was impropriate in the Deans of Ossory. In April 1603, on the death of Queen Elizabeth, St Mary's church was repossessed by the Catholics, and was solemnly re-dedicated by Dr White, Vicar Apostolic of the Diocese of Waterford. A few weeks later, however, it was again reclaimed by the Protestants.[16] By 1615, the church is reported to be 'ruinous', but the chancel was in good condition. In 1642 the church again returned to the Catholics and was reconsecrated. During the eight years of the Confederation of Kilkenny the church remained in Catholic hands. The arrival of Oliver Cromwell in March 1650 brought this to an end. In 1690, during the Jacobite rebellion, the church was used as a magazine.[17]

According to Rev J.B. Leslie, the medieval church was rebuilt before 1731. The rebuilding consisted of taking down the side aisles and the walling-up of the arches on either side. The chancel was shortened within twenty-one feet of the pulpit, and a new east wall was built.[18] Carrigan dates this to 1739 when the vestry books record that '£20 be sessed and levied for ye filling up the arches in ye church and making passages to the two side doors with bricks and plastering and finishing same to make the church warm and staunch'. A view of the church from the north-east shows the rebuilding of the north wall where the chancel was shortened (Plate

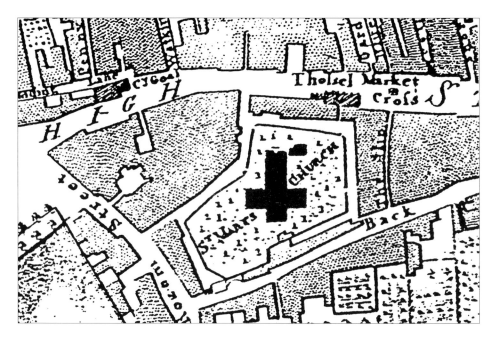

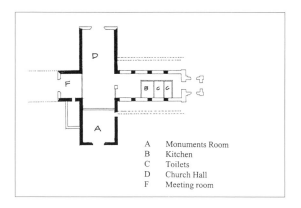

A	Monuments Room
B	Kitchen
C	Toilets
D	Church Hall
F	Meeting room

St Mary's, Kilkenny

10 – A detail of Rocque's map of the town showing the cruciform church of St Mary's with a detached tower

11 – The view from the north-east showing the shortened chancel on the left and the north transept on the right

12 – A plan showing the present arrangements and the surviving thirteenth-century structure (in bold)

11). The intention was not to make the church smaller, but to arrange the interior according to the requirement that everyone could hear the preacher. The same record states 'that Mr. Wm. Watters shall have liberty to erect a gallery at ye north side of the church joining Mr. Lewes' gallery'.[19] These changes are in line with conversions of many other medieval churches to suit the requirements of the 'prayer book church'. In 1753 it is recorded that 'the proprietors of back seats in the old church should ballot for seats in the west aisle of the new church'.[20] The parts of the church which did not fit the pattern of the 'prayer book church', namely the long chancel and the side the aisles, were demolished during the eighteenth century. The north wall of the nave shows where the four-bay arcade to the north aisle was blocked. Three arches were infilled with windows, the one nearest the transept is blocked (*IADS*, ii, pl. 7, 47).

In 1774 the Corporation repaired the steeple of St Mary's, it being in a very ruinous condition. This steeple was taken down in June 1819 when it was replaced by a new steeple and spire, which was finished in 1820. In the *Fourth Report of the Ecclesiastical Commissioners* (1833) the church is described as being 'capable of accommodating 700 persons, enlarged and newly slated in 1819 and a tower and spire added to it in 1826 by means of a loan of £1,107 granted by the Board of First Fruits and by voluntary subscription'. The enlargement is probably the addition of a vestry room to the rear, between the north transept and the shortened chancel.

By 1960, the church was no longer in use and was converted by the Representative Church Body into a parish hall. In 1963 the north transept was converted into a separate 'Monuments Room', into which was placed the important memorials of the church. The monuments room takes up three-quarters of the transept, and is the only part of the building without an inserted floor. This is the only place where the original scale of the building can be appreciated. The conversion of the church into a parish hall was carried out with little regard for the original layout and fabric of the church. A floor was inserted throughout the remainder of the church in order to create a second level of accommodation. On the ground floor there is a parish hall in the south transept and part of the nave (Plate 12). The main body of the nave has been converted into changing rooms and a kitchen. There is a small meeting room in the chancel.

St Mary's church is listed in *Kilkenny, Its Architecture and History*, by Lanigan and Tyler, as a building of national, historical and architectural importance, and is one of ten buildings in Kilkenny included in this category. In the graveyard there are two almshouses, one of which is derelict. Some of the graveyard is surrounded by a hoarding in order to prevent further vandalism of the tombs. The church yard is currently used as a car park.

ST MARY'S, NEW ROSS

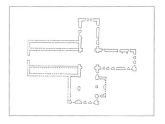

New Ross was an important river port at the junction of the Barrow and the Nore. The town is located on a steep hill, with the church in a prominent position on top of the hill just inside the town wall. The area enclosed by the town walls at New Ross is larger than that enclosed at Drogheda or Kilkenny Hightown, and significantly larger than Waterford whose rival it soon became.[21] St Mary's in New Ross has always been associated with William, Marshal of England, and his wife Isabel de Clare. William, who was also Earl of Pembroke, held title to the lands of Leinster through his wife, who was daughter of Aoife and Strongbow, and granddaughter of Diarmuid Mac Murrough. The chancel of St Mary's was built between 1207 and 1220. The cruciform church originally consisted of a chancel and nave with two aisles and two transepts. St Mary's church represents an important landmark in the history of Irish Gothic architecture. It was the most ambitious parish church of the early thirteenth century, and according to Leask it embodies in simplicity and grace much that was to be characteristic of later Irish structures.

The patronage of the church of New Ross was granted to the canons regular of the Priory of St John in Kilkenny, and their histories were interlinked thereafter. When the Priory of St John in Kilkenny was dissolved, the tithes of the rectory of New Ross were granted to Kilkenny Corporation. Fortunately, New Ross was part of a union of nine parishes, and the incumbent had an income from elsewhere. The Corporation of Kilkenny continued to hold the tithes until the Disestablishment of the Church of Ireland in 1871. In 1684 it is described as having 'a high steeple, crowned in lead, a ring of five bells and a fair pair of organs'.[22] Richard Pococke visited New Ross in 1752, and describes the church as having a handsome tower. In 1759 the steeple of St Mary's was stated to be in ruinous condition and in danger of falling. A subscription was set on foot to have it taken down and rebuilt. In 1763 an additional sum of £200 was voted for the steeple repairs, but by some misfortune it fell.[23] The church is described in *Hibernian Magazine* in 1792 as 'most wretched'.

There is a view of the town of *c*.1799 which shows the church in its dominant position on top of the hill (Plate 13). The steeple is gone, but a short stump of the tower is visible on the west end of the church. The south wall of the nave is seen with a triple arcade to the aisle. Like St Mary's in Kilkenny, the south aisle is gone and the arcade is blocked with smaller windows or doors. The triple lancet window in the south gable of the south transept stands as it does today, but the bell tower on top of the gable is gone. The Corporation of Kilkenny voted £500 in 1800 and £250

St Mary's, New Ross

13 – View of New Ross c.1799 from COPPER PLATE MAGAZINE *(vol. iv) showing the church on the right*

14 – Leask's plan of the church with the vestry and store in the north transept

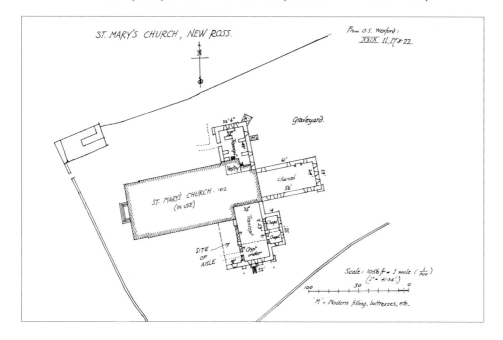

St Mary's, New Ross

15 – A general view from the north-east showing the medieval chancel with the modern church behind

16 – Grose's plan c.1791 showing the west tower and the two aisle arcades

in 1806 towards the repairs of the church.[24] Finally, in 1812, the nave was pulled down and a large church was built on the site. The new church was capable of accommodating a thousand individuals, and was built at a cost of £5,538. The Board of First Fruits granted a loan of £2,676, and the rest was raised by subscription.[25] Hore describes the new church in 1900 as 'but a rude heap of stones and mortar when compared with its predecessor'.[26] Although the nave was pulled down, a considerable amount of the original medieval church remains, including the walls of the chancel and the north and south transepts.

The new church occupies the crossing of the old church, so that the transepts and chancel are all separated from each other and have individual entrances. The south wall of the chancel of the new church now blocks the arch to the south transept. To the left of the photograph the blocked arch to the south aisle can be seen (*IADS*, ii, pl. 16, 60). Leask's undated plan of the church shows a vestry building and store built into the north transept, these structures have since been removed (Plate 14). The south transept has two chapels and a south aisle with a vault underneath. The presence of two large external stone buttresses indicate some structural problems at the north-east corner of the north transept in the past. The position of the new church prevents any physical experience of the connection between remaining sections of the earlier church (Plate 15).

The building of the new church was undertaken with very little regard for the older church. The medieval walls were allowed to remain as long as they did not interfere with the new work. The new church is a fine example of an early eighteenth-century public building, and probably stands on the footprint of the nave of the medieval church. The church is now only used every third Sunday for service, and is the property of the Representative Church Body. The transepts and chancel are national monuments in State care. This division of responsibility for the parts of such a closely intertwined building presents problems for maintenance programmes.

ST MARY'S, THOMASTOWN

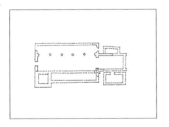

Thomastown was an important medieval river port located on a bridging point of the Nore. The town was founded by Thomas FitzAnthony, who received land in this area from William Marshall in the late twelfth century. The church is sited on the highest point within the town walls, and dates from the mid-thirteenth century. The details of the arcade which survive are similar to St Mary's in Gowran, but executed in a more severe architectural style.[27] FitzAnthony was also the founder of the Augustinian priory at Inistioge, and from the beginning he endowed the priory with the rectorial tithes of the parish of Thomastown. At the Dissolution, the parish church is listed among the possessions of the priory.

The original layout of the church consisted of a chancel and nave with two aisles. The nave and aisles are separated by an arcade, and the five-arch north arcade still survives. The style is Early English Gothic; three of the pillars are quatrefoil in plan and one is circular. The clerestory windows are over the piers rather than the arches. In 1731 Bishop Tennison had reported that 'the church's nave had four arches on one side, five on the other and is unroofed, the chancel is covered and neatly wainscotted and pewed'. In 1732 the chancel was re-roofed and slated. The 'church', which probably meant the chancel only, was still in repair in 1781.[28]

Grose included both a plan of the church and an illustration in his *Antiquities of Ireland*. The plan shows that the church originally consisted of a chancel and a nave with aisles (Plate 16). There is an unusual arrangement with a tower located at the west end of the south aisle. The illustration shows this tower and the nave in a derelict condition (Plate 17). The only part of the church which is roofed is the chancel, which was used as the parish church. The detached chapel to the south of the chancel is also a ruin. Carrigan describes how

> ...thus matters stood till 1809, when the erection of the present Protestant church was decided upon. The site selected for the new structure encroached upon the ground occupied by the ancient church, and the removal of the south aisle and the south wall of the nave of the latter, with all its bays, thus became necessary.

The chancel was also dismantled, presumably to provide materials for the building of the new church. The new church, capable of accommodating 120 people, was completed in 1817, and is described by Lewis as 'a neat modern structure'.[29] The cost of the building was £1,168, all of which was a loan from the Board of First Fruits. When the new church was built, it was placed neatly within the nave of the older church, and it is orientated exactly along the same axis. The importance of occupying the ancient site can be seen in this careful positioning of the church squeezed tightly up against the north arcade. It is curious that one side of the arcade and the chancel were demolished and the other side is retained. There seems to be a deliberate decision to leave just sufficient standing to provide a backdrop, similar to a stage set, to indicate the earlier church (Plate 18).

The 'new' church is no longer in use and has been stripped of all its internal fittings. It is in poor structural condition with cracks in its east gable and south wall, probably as a result of burials. The church is still in the ownership of the Representative Church Body, but there is some discussion at local level about demolishing it in order to provide a better view of the medieval remains. The two churches are physically closely intertwined, and any attempt to demolish the later church would have a strong impact both visually and structurally on the older building. The earlier parts of the church are a national monument in State care.

The entire site is subject to vandalism, and the one remaining effigy still in a wall recess has been enclosed with a steel mesh in order to protect it. As at Callan and New Ross, the modern church is urgently in need of maintenance, while the medieval 'ruined' sections are in reasonable condition.

St Mary's, Thomastown

17 – Grose's view of the church with the nave and west tower in ruins. The chancel is roofed.

*18 – The chancel arch of the medieval church from the south-east
with the modern church on the site of the nave and south aisle*

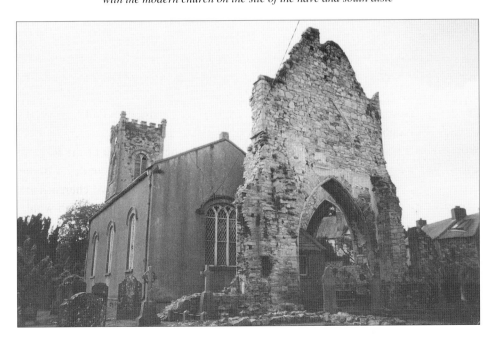

ST LASERIAN'S, LEIGHLIN

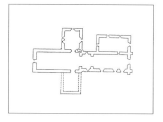

The monastery at Leighlin was founded in the seventh century by St Gobban, but the church is called after his successor, St Laserian. During the church reforms of the twelfth century, it was confirmed the cathedral of the diocese of Leighlin. The present church was probably built by Donatus, who was Bishop of Leighlin between 1152 and 1181. The first Norman bishop, Herlewin, was a Cistercian (c.1202-17). The cathedral was located on the frontier between the Anglo-Norman-controlled lands and the native Irish strongholds of Wicklow. The church was described as situated 'in the middle of a wicked and perverse nation, at the far boundaries of the diocese, in a mountainous, inconvenient and barren place'.[30] In 1248 there was a proposal to relocate it to 'a central safe and fit place in the diocese', presumably east of the Barrow and within the Pale.[31] This relocation was never carried out, and the diocese continued under Anglo-Norman control. The names of the bishops in the thirteenth and fourteenth centuries are all Norman, but Irish names occur again in the fifteenth century.[32]

The cathedral consisted of the long chancel and nave which survive today. The two transepts were built later, to the north and south of the nave. The northern transept is now a roofless ruin, and the southern one has been removed. There is a four-bay sedilia in the south wall beneath these windows, which is reputed to be the only one in Ireland. The later alterations, ascribed to Bishop Matthew Sanders (1529-49), included the insertion of the tower in the west end of the chancel, the addition of the large chapel on the north of the chancel, and the partial rebuilding of the north and south chancel walls. The tower is built on four arches set within the earlier walls, and has an elaborately ribbed vault.[33]

The cathedral returned briefly to Catholic hands during the reign of Queen Mary. Queen Elizabeth nominated the Protestant Daniel Cavanagh as her bishop in 1567.[34] The settlement at Leighlin was eventually superseded by a new one at Leighlin Bridge on a fording point of the river. The status of the cathedral was further undermined in 1832 when the diocese was united with Ferns as a part of the Church Temporalities Act. In the *Fourth Report of the Ecclesiastical Commissioners* (1833), the tithe of the parish, which amounted to £461, was described as 'appropriated to the dean and chapter of Leighlin', and the church declined to parish status with one vicar. Grose's *Antiquities of Ireland* includes an engraving by Barrett, dated September 1792, which shows the church set in the midst of an empty graveyard (Plate 19). The view today has not changed except that the short spire on the tower no longer exists. The Lady chapel, which is ruined in Grose's print with

St Lasarian's, Leighlin

19 – The cathedral from Grose's
ANTIQUITIES OF IRELAND

20 – The buttress built to support the
south wall of the chancel

trees and ivy growing on wall tops and gable, is restored. One of the unusual features of the church is the stepped gable found on both the east and west ends of the church. The steps are most likely the result of the removal of the battlements and wall walks from the wall tops. If this is the case, the wall walks and battlements would have been unusually narrow. The tower has battlements, and as the church was located on the edge of the Pale, the remainder of the church probably had battlements also. The ruined north transept has this stepped-gable feature as well.

The medieval fabric of the building has deteriorated over the centuries. There are large buttresses providing structural support to the north and south walls. The nineteenth-century re-roofing of the church, which included the removal of the collar ties, increased the outward pressure at wall-plate level (Plate 20). The south wall of the chancel shows the top of the wall has moved out, probably as a result of pressure from the roof. The large buttress, which may be built using material from the south transept, crosses one of the chancel windows.

All the resources of the parish have been directed into the upkeep of the chancel, which is warm, bright, carpeted and well maintained. The nave, which is no longer in use for worship, serves as a large foyer to the chancel. It is unheated and faintly illuminated. There is a glazed screen with doors between the redundant nave and the chancel, which is large enough for the present congregation. St Laserian's represents a church caught at a particular stage of decay, preserved at a point where, two hundred years ago, the next step would be the removal of the roof of the nave. St Mary's in Gowran, New Ross, Callan and Thomastown, and St Selskar's in Wexford all went through this stage between the end of the sixteenth century and the eighteenth century. The roofs on the chapter house, nave and the chancel are in good condition. The ruined north transept has been abandoned. The openings have been bricked up and the wall tops are covered in vegetation. There are two fonts in the cathedral. The one standing in the chancel, which is in use, dates from the thirteenth century, while the one standing by the main door dates from AD 1225, when it was originally installed in St Mary's Church, Gowran. When the church in Gowran was closed, the church authorities moved the font to St Laserian's.

THE PRIORY OF INISTIOGE

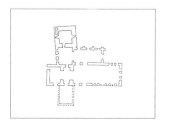

The town of Inistioge is located on a ford (and later a bridge) across the river Nore, between Thomastown and New Ross. The monastic tradition at this site dates back to the early Christian period, and is associated with St Colmcille. The Augustinian Priory of St Columba was founded in c.1206 by the Anglo-

Norman Thomas fitz Anthony, Seneschal of Leinster. Inistioge was a walled town, but the exact location of the walls is not known. Fitz Anthony made ample provision for the support of the new priory, endowing it with the entire village of Inistioge and several townlands, together with the fishery of the river Nore for a length of about three miles. He granted the priory the rectories or parishes of Inistioge, Grenan (now the civil parish of Thomastown), and Kilcrenath (now Dunkitt).[35] The nearby Augustinian priory in Kells supplied at least one of the priors of Inistioge, named Alured. However, relationships between the two foundations were not always cordial. In 1355 Stephen de Kerlyon, prior of Kells, was alleged to have robbed John Modbury, prior of Inistioge.[36]

In the early sixteenth century, Milo Baron, who was also the Bishop of Ossory, was prior at Inistioge. He built a new steeple and cloister, and surrendered the priory in 1540. The dating of the cloister is probably between c.1510 and 1528, and is one of the last medieval cloisters to be built in Ireland.[37] The church was drawn by Richard Langrishe for the *Journal of the Royal Society of Antiquaries of Ireland* (*JRSAI*) in 1874. The plan shows a chancel church with a crossing tower and an extremely short nave (Plate 21). The north transept is shown at a slight angle to the tower connecting to another tower, which is known as the Black Castle. There is a Lady chapel between the north transept and the chancel. Langrishe also indicates by a lighter hatching the possible location of the cloister and the south transept. The priory at Inistioge presents an unusual arrangement with a short nave in comparison to the chancel. Langrishe's drawing is difficult to read and the lettering is illegible.

Leask describes the Black Castle as a 'curious octagonal tower on a square base with no easily datable features', but suggests it may date from the thirteenth century. If the Black Castle is earlier than the rest it would explain the asymmetrical relationship between the tower and the north transept. The unusually short nave may be due to the fact that Milo Baron never completed the work of extending the nave, either because he became bishop in 1528 or the Dissolution intervened in 1540. There is a roof scar on the crossing tower which indicates that there was a south transept (*IADS*, ii, pl. 17, 60). Following the Dissolution, in 1541, the jurors reported that the priory church was 'parochial', and that all other buildings with orchards and gardens within the precincts were necessary for the farmer. The priory, including the interest in fourteen rectories, was granted in 1566 to Sir Edmond Butler whose father was James, 9th Earl of Ormond.[38] The estate eventually passed to William Tighe who converted the prior's tower, or Black Castle, into a family mausoleum in 1874.

There is an illustration of the priory dating from about 1770 in *The Dublin Sunday Magazine* which shows the chancel of the church in ruins with ivy growing over the walls (Plate 22). The adjoining Lady chapel is shown neatly roofed, and

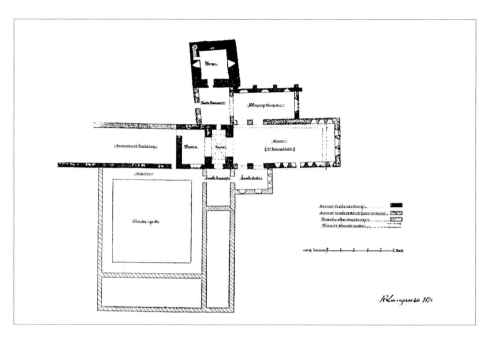

The Priory Church of Inistioge

*21 – Richard Langrish's plan in
JRSAI, 1896*

*22 – A drawing of the priory from
the east by Seymour, c.1770, from
THE DUBLIN SUNDAY MAGAZINE*

*23 – The modern church built in
1825 is on the left. The ruins of the
Lady chapel are on the right.*

was used as a Protestant church until 1824. The Black Castle stands to the right of the Lady chapel. In 1825 the chancel of the old church was demolished and a new church was built on the site, capable of accommodating 200 people. The church cost £1,169, and a grant of £830 was given by way of a gift and £276 by way of a loan by the Board of First Fruits. The remainder was supplied by a donation from the Rt Hon W.F. Tighe.[39] When building the new church in 1824, the walls of the Lady chapel were cut back, in a similar fashion to Callan, to allow the new walls to be built (Plate 23). The older structure was treated with little respect, with the new vestry built into the north transept, almost blocking access the Lady chapel.

In his article in the *JRSAI* Langrishe looks back at events in 1824 from his post-Gothic revival position of 1896, and describes how 'the mode of restoration adopted was to pull down the choir entirely, and to erect the present building in imitation of it. Unfortunately no architect seems to have known better in that degenerate period.' Despite his disapproval of the demolition of the chancel, Langrishe describes how the Rev James Graves 'found in the old church in Kells a fine twelfth-century font with one side carved; the others had been left plain'.[40] The Rev James asked one of the stone carvers involved in the restoration of St Canice's Cathedral to carve the other three sides to match the first one. 'This most suitable gift', the Kell's font, was presented by Mr Langrishe to the W.F. Tighe, as he had been a munificent benefactor of the restoration of the cathedral.

One of the interesting aspects of this study is the relationship between the Catholic and Protestant church. A new Roman Catholic church was built in the nineteenth century on the site of the cloister and as close as possible to the original monastic church. This shows the desire of the Catholics to repossess the ancient sites. Many fragments of carved stone were unearthed during the building of the Catholic church, and several panels are built into the wall of the church yard. The graveyard located between the two churches is strewn with carved stone from the vanished cloister. There is more carved stone at a 'holy well' situated above the village. Both churches are in use today.

THE PRIORY CHURCH OF ST JOHN, KILKENNY

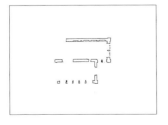

Kilkenny was the site of an important early Christian monastic site and the administrative centre of the kings of Ossory. The city is located on a bridging point of the river Nore, and the Anglo-Normans established a borough here in 1176. The Priory of St John is located on the far bank of the river, where settlement was initiated shortly after 1200. This settlement was enclosed by a separate wall and was connected to the rest of the city via St John's Bridge. The priory was founded in 1211 by William Marshall for the canons regular of St Augustine, but the monks continued to reside in their earlier foundation near John's Bridge until 1325. In 1227, William Marshall, the 2nd Earl of Pembroke, appropriated the parish church of St Evin and New Ross with the chapel of the Blessed Virgin to St John's, Kilkenny. In 1230, Peter, Bishop of Ossory, granted the priory part of the tithe of the church or rectory of Claragh. The priory continued to prosper, and about 1290 an elaborate Lady chapel was built on the southern side of the chancel. The layout of the church and the priory is not known, but in 1315 the bell tower of the priory church fell.

The priory continued to gather tithes from the surrounding area, and by about 1350 its possessions included the parishes of 'Jeryponte, St John's with Loghmetheran, Dromerthir, Claragh, Kilmelag, Dunfert, Tibretbretayn, Kildrey-nagh, McCully, Castlecomer and Scatheryk (Skirke)'.[41] In 1374, the prior was confirmed in the possession of the church or parish of Castlecomer by Alexander Balscot, Bishop of Ossory. Edmond Comeford was the prior of St John's in 1506, he was also the Bishop of Ferns and the Dean of Ossory. In 1540, Richard Cantwell, the last prior of St John's, surrendered the priory and all its possessions to Henry VIII. A portion of the possessions, together with the priory itself, was granted to the mayor and citizens of Kilkenny.[42] The church was deemed to have been 'parochial', and Richard Cantwell was appointed curate and chaplain of the parochial church of St John the Evangelist, Kilkenny, 'receiving the third part of the church, rectory or chapel aforesaid (St John the Evangelist) and also the third part of all tithes together with a house and garden in Kilkenny'.[43] By 1615, the church and chancel were in ruins and the Corporation was ordered to repair it.[44]

In 1645, during the time of the Confederation of Kilkenny, Thomas Rothe, a secular priest, Dean and Vicar-general of Ossory, was appointed commendatory prior of St John's abbey. The Jesuit fathers were made a grant of the priory, confirmed by the Nuncio Rinuccini, to use the site for a college or seminary.[45] After Cromwell's capture of Kilkenny in 1650, the Jesuits were driven out of St John's priory. Forty years later, during the reign of James II, the Jesuits applied to the Corporation to be restored to the priory, but in the meantime the Capuchins had taken over a plot in the priory grounds and the Corporation were reluctant to move them. However, within a few years, the Catholic Corporation was disbanded and both the Jesuits and the Capuchins were banished. In 1731 Bishop Tennison reported, 'here are seen the ruins of a very large church, a vestry room still remaining. An old masshouse and 3 Popish Priests, two popish schoolmasters. 460 Protestants, 1,366 Papists.'[46] In about 1780, the nave of the church, with its two square towers,

The Priory Church of St John, Kilkenny

*24 – William Robertson's illustration of the Lady chapel, c.1813
– the impressive east window is shown with its lower section blocked*

25 – Robertson's proposed restoration, c.1813

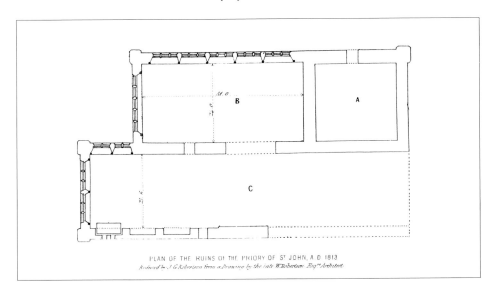

PLAN OF THE RUINS OF THE PRIORY OF ST JOHN, A.D. 1813

ABBEY OF SAINT JOHN IN KILKENNY.

St John's, Kilkenny

26a – A drawing of the south wall of the Lady chapel from the National Library before rebuilding

26b – A photograph of the south wall as rebuilt

27 – A plan of the church showing the parts of the structure in State care (in bold)

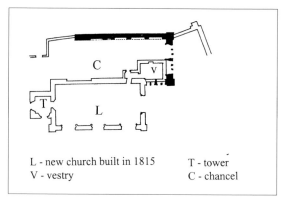

L - new church built in 1815   T - tower
V - vestry   C - chancel

and the domestic buildings were knocked down and the materials used to construct a nearby infantry barracks.[47]

By 1780 only the chancel, Lady chapel, and the base of a tower remained of the original church. The Lady chapel was widely known as 'the lantern of Ireland', due to the elaborate traceried windows which filled the entire east gable wall and south wall of the church. There are several contemporary illustrations of this wonder, including one in Grose's *Antiquities of Ireland* (*c*.1791). In this illustration the Lady chapel is in ruins, but five triple windows fill the south wall, and the east window fills the entire gable wall. Grose describes this as 'about sixteen feet wide and thirty high'. Another engraving from this period, this time by J. Walker, shows the chancel and the Lady chapel with a large, open archway between. The windows in the east gables are shown partially blocked, and the engraving is accompanied by a description of the ruins, which 'extend through several gardens and adjoining yards on the banks of the river, where many antique monuments and vestiges of the cloister still remain preserved'.

The Kilkenny architect William Robertson also recorded St John's about 1813. He included two views of the interior of the ruins – one of the Lady chapel and the other of the chancel. In his view of the Lady chapel, the impressive east window is shown with the lower section blocked (Plate 24). On the north wall of the Lady chapel there is a belfry on top of the wall, and at the base there is a tomb niche with a canopy arch. This niche is now built into the boundary wall of the graveyard. Robertson's second view, the interior of the chancel, shows the fine east window surviving today (*IADS*, ii, pls 18-19, 61). The south wall of the chancel has a pair of windows that also survive, as do the three plain tomb niches shown on the left. The ground level in the chancel seems to be considerably higher than that in the Lady chapel to the right. There are two further niches, with a canopy arch overhead, in the south wall of the Lady chapel.

In 1815 the Corporation of Kilkenny granted a lease of the 'two chancels and the churchyard' of St John's to the vicar Robert Shaw and two of the churchwardens in order that 'a church might be built on the site for the use and benefit of the Protestant inhabitants of the parish'.[48] William Robertson undertook the restoration of the ruins, and in an article in the *JRSAI*, his proposed plans are reproduced (Plate 25). He was 'very anxious to preserve the entire of the ruins and sepulchral monuments', and proposed that the chancel was used as the parish church (marked C on the plan), that a groined entrance porch was provided for the church (marked A), and the Lady chapel was roofed with the intention of having it form a receptacle for the ancient tombs and other relics of ornamental sculpture lying about the ruins (marked B).[49] In this drawing it is not clear if all the structure shown is the surviving medieval church, but if this is correct, there was a tower at the west end of the Lady chapel. Robertson's proposals were rejected by the vestry on account of the expense involved, and the 're-building and re-roofing of the Lady Chapel alone' was determined upon by the parochial authorities. Mr Robertson's views having been frustrated, he declared himself 'not to be held accountable for the present rather incongruous arrangement, and the sad havoc made amongst the ancient tombs'.[50] The new church was built in 1815 at a cost of £1,246, of which sum £369 was granted as a gift and £553 as a loan from the Board of First Fruits. The residue was raised by private subscription.[51] Mr Robertson continued as architect for the project, and he describes how 'the ruin of the Lady chapel was taken down for the purpose of building a church, the front wall (which contained the famous arcade of five triplets) was inclined above fourteen inches out of the perpendicular and the entire height did not exceed twenty feet, yet non of the mullions had fallen.'[52] The wall was rebuilt and much of the original carvings was replaced with copies. The attempt to reproduce the earlier façade did not extend as far as replacing the five windows which had been the main glory of the original chapel. Three of the five windows were replaced, with the area in-between blocked with masonry (Plate 26). Inside the church the original thirteenth-century windows were retained, but outside the original carvings were replaced by accurate copies of the original. The location of the medieval stone carvings discarded during the project is not known. The east window of the Lady chapel, which had filled the gable, also disappeared, and it was replaced by a considerably smaller window which resembles a section of the earlier one.

The location of the vestry and coal store was handled in a similar fashion to New Ross (in the north transept), Thomastown (directly against the arcade) and Inistioge (in the north transept). In St John's, the vestry and coal store are built in the adjoining chancel (*IADS*, ii, pl. 19, 61). The building of the vestry required the blocking up of the lower sections of both the south and east windows of the chancel. The vestry roof prevents proper access to the windows for conservation work.

Since 1933 the chancel of the medieval church is a national monument in State care. The area in guardianship is shown on the plan of the modern church (Plate 27). The modern church, including the vestry and store in the chancel, are the responsibility of the Representative Church Body. As in the case of St Mary's in New Ross, it is difficult to carry out a satisfactory conservation programme to the medieval part of the church. The church is still in use as a Church of Ireland parish church, and is in good condition. The interior of the church was reordered in 1871, and still retains its fixtures and fittings from that time. The chancel is in poor condition; the presence of the vestry and coal store are visually intrusive and prevent proper access to the east and south windows. At present, there is no public right of way into the chancel.

THE PRIORY CHURCH OF SS PETER & PAUL (SELSKAR), WEXFORD

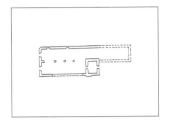

Wexford is located on a ferry point of the Slaney river where it enters the sea. The city was founded by Norse settlers on the south shore of the bay, but was taken by the Anglo-Normans in 1169. The church of the Augustinian Priory of SS Peter & Paul (commonly called Selskar's) is located just inside the town walls, beside the west gate. Part of the priory may have been outside the walls.[53] The foundation date of the priory is unknown, but it seems likely that it was established *c*.1216. Sir Alexander des Roche was its patron. On 24 January 1541, the jurors of the Dissolution reported that the priory church had been a parish church from time immemorial.[54] The monastery was described as holding the advowsons or interests in twenty-one rectories and vicarages.

The ruins today consist of an unusual arrangement of a naved church with a tower at the east end of the south aisle. The rectangular tower dates from the fourteenth century. It has quoins of imported Somersetshire stone with a projecting turret that accommodates the spiral stairs. There is also a nave with a four-arched south aisle arcade supported on two rectangular and one hexagonal pier. The west gable walls of both aisle and nave stand to full height, together with two arches of the arcade. The west window of the nave is pointed, and originally held a five-light traceried window. The west gable of the aisle also held a pointed window. Excavations carried out in 1973 found traces of a rood screen, and also revealed that the thirteenth-century nave had originally been built without aisles. The tower had probably been built at the same time as the aisle was built.[55]

There is an illustration of the church in Grose's *Antiquities of Ireland* (vol. 2) which shows the church in ruins (Plate 28). The chancel is shown with the eastern gable wall standing to full height with a round-headed window and two windows in the south wall. The battlements of the tower are shown in poor condition, and in the background the gateway on the town wall is visible.

In the early years of the nineteenth century, the Established Church authorities decided to reuse the site for worship. The ruins of the chancel were demolished to accommodate a new church built between 1818 and 1826 and consecrated in 1826. The new church was not built on the site of the chancel, but instead on the southern side of it, carefully centered on the existing tower. The construction of the new church cost £1,384, of which £830 was a gift and the remainder was a loan from the Board of First Fruits. An illustration by Anne Wylie shows the church around 1840 (Plate 29). The new church is a handsome Gothic Revival building with carefully detailed stone features. It is a more complex structure than the stan-

The Priory Church of SS Peter & Paul (Selskar), Wexford

28 – *An illustration from Grose's* ANTIQUITIES OF IRELAND
showing the church in ruins

29 – *Anne Wylie's illustration, c.1840*

dard 'box with square tower' associated with the Board of First Fruits. In my opinion, the church is undoubtedly the work of John Semple who was employed as an architect by the Board of First Fruits from 1825 until 1831.[56] The church is similar in detail to those built by Semple at Feighcullen, Co Kildare, and Tallaght, Co Dublin. Semple is known to have built fourteen churches for the Board, but St Selskar's has not previously been included.

An examination of the stone work of the new church shows that a substantial amount of the stone from the demolished chancel was reused in the new work (*IADS*, ii, pl. 15, 59). There is a clear difference between the large square granite stone used in the base of the walls and the red sandstone used higher up the walls. A commentator in 1915 describes the ruins as 'well worthy of a visit, and the tower is still in good preservation. The beauty of the spot is marred by a modern Protestant church.'[57] The new church was part of St Patrick's Union of fourteen churches, and remained in use until the 1960s. The older part of the ruins, consisting of the nave and aisle, was passed into State guardianship in 1947, while the remainder, including the tower and the nineteenth-century church, passed into State guardianship in 1970. The Representative Church Body removed the roof and all internal fittings and furniture prior to handing over the church. The locations of the memorial plaques can be seen by marks left in the plaster. Conservation work was undertaken at the site in 1972. The works consisted of wall-top flaunching in the nave, resetting of copings, removal of rubble and blocking of dangerous openings at the west end. Works to the tower consisted of repointing, flaunching and general repairs to the masonry. A total of £6,000 was spent at the site, making it a 'major work' lasting until 1973.[58] There is no mention of any work carried out on the later church. Conservation work to date has focused on the medieval parts of the church, and little attention has been paid to the nineteenth-century ruin.

DUISKE, OR GRAIGUENAMANAGH ABBEY CHURCH

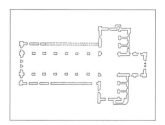

Duiske Abbey was founded in about 1204 by William Marshall, Earl of Pembroke, who acquired extensive territory in Leinster. Monks from the mother house in Stanly in Wiltshire were brought over to start this Anglo-Norman foundation. The abbey was located on the banks of the river Barrow in an isolated valley. The building of the monastery began in 1204 and was probably finished about 1230 to 1240.[59] Duiske is one of the finest examples in Ireland of the early English style of architecture. The church is cruciform in shape, with symmetrical aisles to the seven-bay nave and three chapels to each arm of the transept. It is identical in plan, and very nearly in dimension, to that of Strata Florida Abbey in Cardiganshire, which was partly completed by 1201. Its total over-all length is 64.65m, and it measures nearly 36.6m over the transept. It is the largest of the Irish Cistercian churches and, with its claustral buildings (which surrounded a garth of 36 square metres), the largest abbey of the order in Ireland.[60] The tower was part of the original design and was carried on four enormous arches, of which only one remains. The piers of the seven bays of the nave were square in plan with the clerestory windows over the piers, according to the Irish fashion.

The monastery was dissolved by Henry VIII in 1536. The abbot, Charles O'Cavanagh was granted a pension of £10, and the site and the other possessions were granted to James, Earl of Ormond, in January 1538. In 1541 the jurors found that 'the site of two acres contained a church, a cemetery, several granges, many cottages, three water mills, four eel-weirs, with an interest in five rectories, total value given as £76. But much property was undervalued being waste, unoccupied or in ruins.' [61] The story of Duiske from 1541 to 1691 is closely allied with the family history of the Butlers. Tradition says that one actually built a residence in the nave of the church, and was thereafter commonly referred to as 'Mr. Piers Butler of the Abbey'. The last Butler to possess Duiske was Piers Butler, the 3rd Lord Galmoy, who fought at the Boyne, Aughrim and Limerick, and became one of the 'Wild Geese'. He died without issue in 1740.[62]

By 1729 the roof had fallen, and a 'mass house' was erected against the outer walls. In 1774 the tower collapsed, bringing with it two of the four great arches underneath and the groin vaulted roof of the chancel. The cloisters, scriptorium and refectory were all incorporated into the buildings and gardens of the town.[63] The earliest illustration of the abbey is from Beranger's *Views of Ireland*, and dates to about 1776, about fifty years after the tower fell (Plate 31). In this view, the claustral buildings are shown roofed and obviously in use. The chancel and the north transept are both in ruins. There is a small building with a thatch roof (possibly the mass house) erected against the side of the north transept. The nave, which is just glimpsed behind the transept, is roofed. This roofed nave is probably the Protestant church, which was fitted up in 1754.[64] The building was most likely leased from the owner. Grose includes two views of the ruins dated 1792. The external view of the chancel and the north transept is similar to Beranger's. Grose describes the ruins 'of great extent, and the architecture and sculpture, even in its present ruined state, excite our admiration'. William Robertson has two views of the monastery which date from *c*.1815. The internal view shows the north transept and the chancel, with one of the two surviving arches of the tower (Plate 30). In 1807, the Established Church decided to build a new church and school a short distance away at White-

Duiske, Co Kilkenny

30 – William Robertson's illustration of the interior of the chancel c.1815

31 – The earliest illustration of the abbey, showing the claustral buildings roofed and the chancel and north transept in ruins, from Beranger's VIEWS OF IRELAND, c.1776

32 – Duiske, Co Kilkenny
the view from the nave towards the altar, underneath the crossing

hall. They took down the roof erected in 1754 for incorporation into the new church.[65] A description of the church from this time by John Bernard Trotter described the ruins in 1812: 'I cannot describe how nobly venerable it looked. I do not except the celebrated Abbey of Tintern in Monmouthshire when I say that nothing could be found more venerable and beautifully interesting in the empire than Graingnamanagh [*sic*] Abbey.'[66]

From 1813 the church was re-roofed and used for Catholic worship. This project was undertaken against the backdrop of the tithe wars and the gradual recovery of the fortunes of the Catholic community. The parishioners, under the direction of the parish priest, the Rev Louis Moore, re-roofed the greater part of the church, rebuilt the walls where they had collapsed (the walls of the nave towards the west remained standing, but the section towards the crossing had fallen), and added three galleries. At the same time, the debris from the fallen tower was spread over the floor space to a depth of about five feet.[67] In 1886 the western part was roofed over. The damaged arches were repaired and joined to the gable of the present church. A bell was installed the following year, and 'this event caused much rejoicing when its mellow tones first echoed over the valley at Christmas 1887'.[68]

The church continued to be used by the Catholic community for the next hundred years. By the early 1970s the church was in need of extensive and costly repairs. Percy le Clerc, who had been an inspector of national monuments and who had directed the work at Rothe House, Ballintubber Abbey and Holy Cross, was commissioned to prepare plans and estimates for the work, including the removal of the galleries, the reordering of the interior, the removal of the blocking of the arcades, and the construction of a new roof at the original line of the gable. The decision to restrict work to a 'sympathetic adaptation of the medieval church leaving the original fabric unaltered' rather than a full-scale restoration was based on the available resources.[69] The demolition of the roof and galleries began in 1974. While clearing the way for rebuilding wall supports for the new roof in the chancel, the exit from the staircase leading to the tower and apartments over the groined arches of the choir was discovered. Stripped of the galleries and furnishings, a clear picture of the massive church could be appreciated (Plate 32). The circular rose window was opened, and on either side two additional window openings could be seen. These, like the window in the north transept, were badly damaged by the removal of part of the window in 1813 to lay the low pitched roof.[70] There is a viewing point where the original medieval floor can be seen in situ at least five feet below the present level. The restored church is so large that the interior has been reordered, with the altar now located under the crossing in order to reduce the distance between the congregation and the priest. The chancel has a separate altar that can be used for more intimate services. The side chapels on the south transept are also used for small services.

The history of this church serves to confirm the belief that if the Protestant congregations abandoned the ancient places of worship, they would be repossessed by the Catholics. The reason they succeeded in this instance is due to the fact that the church was not declared to be 'parochial' at the Dissolution, and passed into lay hands. The Established Church used the church for worship, probably holding a lease until 1807. The persistence and commitment of the Catholic community in roofing the church in 1813 is contrasted by the well-endowed Protestant community supported by the Board of First Fruits. The survival of the medieval church may be due to the overwhelming scale of the surviving elements that, by the end of the eighteenth century, were universally recognised as 'romantic' and of some value.

The symbolic importance of the church to the Catholics can be seen here where the site is first colonised by a mass house built up against the walls and eventually regained. The descriptions of the recent restoration of the church are triumphantly described with an emphasis on continuity with the past. The church is in good condition today and in daily use.

BALTINGLASS MONASTERY CHURCH

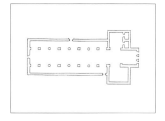

In 1148 Dermot MacMurrough, King of Leinster, brought Cistercian monks to Baltinglass from Mellifont to found a new monastery which he called 'The Valley of Salvation'. The foundation at Baltinglass, located in the western foothills of the Wicklow mountains, was one of the first wave of the expansion of the Cistercians in Ireland. Baltinglass in turn was the mother-house of a number of other Cistercian foundations, including Jerpoint, founded in 1160, Abbeymahon in 1172, Monasterevan in 1178, and Abbeyleix in 1184. Baltinglass was not an Anglo-Norman foundation, although Dermot MacMurrough was later closely associated with the Anglo-Normans and his daughter married Strongbow. Baltinglass was located on the edge of the Pale, on the western borders of the O'Byrne and O'Toole strongholds in Wicklow, and the abbey maintained a strong Irish identity. The location of the monastery at the frontier gave it a strategic importance as a military outpost. The monastery was the centre of a number of disputes in the thirteenth century, one in which the monks were accused of harbouring 'felons against the English'.[71]

The church was cruciform in plan, consisting of a nave with aisles, chancel and two transepts. The building was probably complete about 1180, with the tower inserted in the crossing at a later date. The church is almost as large as Duiske but the carvings have a distinct Irish character. The north arcade of the nave is gone, but the eight-bay south arcade still stands. The piers are alternatively square and circular in plan, and all but one rises from low walls now broken away in the openings. The capitals of the piers are boldly carved with simple Irish motifs. Peter Harbison describes the decorative carved stone at Baltinglass as 'showing an interesting fusion of Cistercian and Irish Romanesque architecture'.

After the Suppression in 1541, the jurors found in the precinct 'a very ruinous church' to which the parishioners resorted. They also found on the site 'a castle, hall with chamber, and a very ruinous kitchen, all unvalued. There were some 2,300 acres of land, several unmeasured holdings, with castles or manors, granges, many messuages and cottages, mills, and an interest in a number of churches',[72] with a total value entered at £126. The property was granted, with other monasteries, to Sir Edmond Butler in 1556. The church was deemed to be 'parochial', and continued to be used for worship. In 1793 there is an illustration in Grose's *Antiquities of Ireland* showing the later-inserted crossing tower standing to full height (Plate 33). The tower, which has a curious set-back on the north face, is roofed and topped with a structure that probably housed the bell. The roof scar of the nave is visible, but there is a smaller, shorter building intruding into the nave which incorporates the first arch of the north aisle arcade on the north wall of this structure. The west wall of the north transept stands almost to full height, and the archway from the transept into the north aisle is also visible. The chancel, which is just glimpsed behind, is roofed. The south arcade and the west wall stand as they do today. The principal change between Grose's view from 1793 and 1815 was the destruction of the crossing tower. The building intruding into the nave was retained, and a square tower was added on to the west end (*IADS*, ii, pl. 1, 26). The arches of the crossing tower were retained on the two east-west walls, but were removed where they crossed the new church on the north-south axis. Together with Callan, this is the only example among the case studies where the original chancel is used for worship, and not demolished and rebuilt.

The *Fourth Report of the Ecclesiastical Commissioners* of 1833 states that the living is a rectory with an income is £618 per annum, all of which is derived from the tithe of the parish. The church was capable of holding five hundred people. There is no record of a loan from the Board of First Fruits, but £27 was raised by the Exclusive Vestry for keeping the church in repair, and £6 for erecting a new

33 – Baltinglass Monastery, from Grose's ANTIQUITIES OF IRELAND

gallery. In his *Topographical Dictionary*, Lewis reports that 'in 1815, at an expense of £500, the church which occupies the site of the chancel of an ancient abbey was repaired and a square tower added to it. A grant of £252 had "lately" been made by the Ecclesiastical Commissioners for its further repair.' [73] In 1883, the church in the chancel was abandoned when a new church was built beside the ancient ruin. This move was due to the desire for a comfortable building rather than any great concern with the principals of Morris and Ruskin. The new church was built with the stone from the 'Abbot's castle' to the south-east, which was demolished in 1882 by the rector to provide materials for the construction of the new parish church and a glebe house.[74] The new church was built in the Gothic Revival style, and the abandoned church became a national monument in State care. The church in the chancel was dismantled and the roof of the tower was removed.

Baltinglass illustrates the change brought about by the introduction of the Irish Church Act. At the start of the nineteenth century the Church of Ireland was compelled to remain at the site of the Abbey. However, by the end of the century, as a result of legislation which effectively prevented any worship at the site, the Church of Ireland could relocate and build a more convenient building. The ruins are in a reasonable condition today.

THE BLACK ABBEY, KILKENNY

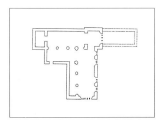

The Black Abbey was founded by William Marshall, the younger, in 1225. It was the third Irish house for the Dominican order, after Dublin and Drogheda. The abbey was located on the banks of the Bregagh river, just outside the walls of the new Anglo-Norman settlement of Hightown in Kilkenny and just below the older settlement of Irishtown centred on the Cathedral of St Canice. The abbey prospered, and five general chapters of the order were held there between 1281 and 1349. In 1337 the Corporation entrusted the keys and custody of the 'Blackfreren Gate' to the Dominicans.[75] During the great plague of Kilkenny in 1349, eight friars died within a period of three months. As a result of their destitute conditions, the Corporation, in 1352, allowed the friars the rents of two houses to provide hosts and wine for daily mass. The finances of the abbey improved in 1437 when King Henry VI granted the friars two parts of the tithes of the rectory of Mothel.[76] In 1487 a Dominican named Oliver Cantwell became Bishop of Ossory, a post he held for almost forty years. He had close connections with the Shortall family who were responsible for the insertion of the central tower at the junction of the chancel, nave and transept.

The remains of the abbey church do not conform to the standard arrangements of Anglo-Norman foundations. The churches of the Dominicans were 'assembled over time – the diversity of junctions and the ensuing unresolved, additive quality becoming one of the chief characteristics of the type'.[77] The original church consisted of a chancel, a nave with a south aisle, and a western tower. The remarkably long south transept, which is easily as large as the nave, was added about 1324. The south window with its elaborate tracery is the largest of its type, filling almost the whole of the south gable wall. The plan of the Black Abbey provides a remarkable contrast to both Baltinglass and Graiguenamanagh. The unity of style which is associate with the Cistercian foundations is entirely absent in the Black Abbey. The Cistercians built their abbeys, according to a preordained layout, in one main phase of construction, but the Black Abbey is typical of the ad hoc style of the mendicant friars. The churches of these foundations, representing a middle ground between the austere monasteries and the regular clergy, evolved over many years. The crossing tower is usually not centred on the transept, but located, as at the Black Abbey, further to the east. Sherkin Abbey, Kilcrea Abbey and Timoleague Abbey, all Franciscan foundations in Co Cork, display these features. There is a marked lack of symmetry and order.

The addition of the transept with its west aisle transformed the rectangular shaped building into a T-shape. The tower is inserted between the nave and the chancel but is not centred on the south transept. As a result, when viewed from the end of the transept, the south crossing arch is half visible to the right, and the first arch of the south arcade of the nave is to the left. The tower is of early sixteenth-century date. In 1543 the abbey was dissolved and its possessions were granted to the sovereign and to the burgesses and commonality of Kilkenny and to their successors forever.[78] After the Suppression, the church was converted into a courthouse. The Dominicans remained on in Kilkenny, and obviously did not relinquish their hopes of regaining the abbey. In 1603, when the news of Elizabeth's death reached Kilkenny, three Dominicans, with the help of townspeople, broke open the doors of the abbey, pulled down the bars and benches, and set up an altar for the celebration of Mass.[79] During the Confederation of Kilkenny from 1642 to 1649, the Black Abbey again returned to Catholic hands. A public ordination was held there by the papal nuncio, Rinunccini. When Cromwell arrived in March 1650 the Dominicans were ejected. The Dominicans remained on in Kilkenny, and there are records of priors in 1663 and in 1667. The Duke of Ormond complained in 1683 of their insolence and indiscretion fitting up four chapels at Kilkenny.[80] The building continued to be used as a church by the Catholics until June 1694 when the Protestant bishop complained to the Lord Deputy that, 'Even on Sunday last they set their mass pub-

The Black Abbey, Kilkenny

34 – The Black Abbey, from Grose's ANTIQUITIES OF IRELAND

*35 – The Black Abbey today from the south-west,
with the south transept on the right*

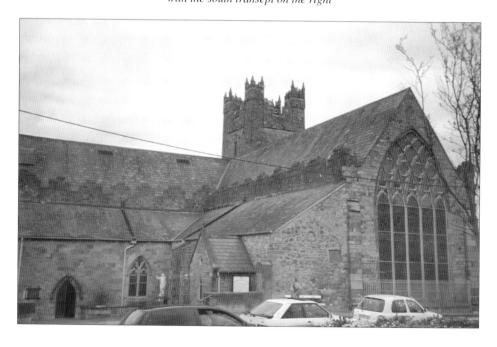

licly on foot again in their late hallowed abbey in Kilkenny; which they undertook to the Lord Lieutenant to alter to a session-house, as it formally was.'[81] The abbey was again returned to use as a courthouse and the sovereign was thrown into prison. By 1744 there were no Dominicans left in Kilkenny. In 1776, a Dominican curate, in an attempt to regain the abbey, became the tenant of the lease holder. In 1788 Fr Shaw succeeded in roofing the transept and repairing the walls, but the bishop forbade its use as a church as he felt that there were enough chapels in Kilkenny already.

Grose's *Antiquities of Ireland* included two views of the abbey from 1793. The external view shows that the entire abbey is ruined (Plate 34). The transept and tower stand to full height, as they do today. The west tower is shown standing to its full height. The chancel is still standing but is in poor condition, with large holes in the south wall where the cut-stone window surrounds have been robbed. The east gable, with three lancet windows, stands to full height. The marked difference between the condition of the transept with all its battlements complete and the chancel may be due to Fr Shaw's efforts at restoration. Around the perimeter of the church are clusters of thatched cabins. The Dominicans continued to hold the lease on the church but did not use it for worship until 1816 when Fr Gavin, against the wishes of his bishop, celebrated public Mass in the roofed transept of the abbey. Following this rebellion he was replaced by another priest, John Prendergast, who was given strict instructions never to open the church again. Despite this order, by 1850 there was a committee for the 'repairs of the Black Abbey' in existence. In 1859 J.J. McCarthy was engaged in making plans for the entire restoration, although no drawings of the church survive. In 1864 the restored church was rededicated (Plate 35).

The present building consists of a nave with a south aisle of about the thirteenth century, a south transept also with an aisle built about 1330, a crossing tower inserted in 1527, and a west tower of fifteenth-century date. The claustral buildings extended north of the abbey, with the river Breagagh forming the boundary. The present church was restored in 1976 when the area underneath the tower that was used as a sacristy was opened up. The transept and the nave are both used for worship today, and the church is in good condition and is well maintained. The church passed through a familiar history of ruination and restoration. The major destruction was the chancel and the top of the west tower, but the rest has survived in good condition. The history of the Black Abbey provides proof of the importance of the possession of the ancient places of worship and the desire for continuity with the past.

———

CATHOLIC RESURGENCE AND THE IRISH CHURCH ACT

The history of the churches show that despite declining numbers, the Church of Ireland possessed the majority of the ancient churches and actively restored for use those that had become derelict. The churches at St John's in Kilkenny, St Selskar's in Wexford and St Mary's in Callan had all become ruins before their restorations in 1813, 1826 and 1837 respectively. The two medieval churches which had not been declared 'parochial' by the jurors following the Dissolution of the monasteries were regained by the Roman Church. The first step was the establishment of a foothold by building a mass house against the outer walls. The restoration of Duiske began in 1813 and continued through most of the nineteenth century. The case of the Black Abbey suggests that the desire to regain the site was beyond reach of practical argument.

During the second half of the nineteenth century the Catholic Church undertook an impressive building programme, acquiring new sites in prominent locations. The Church of Ireland gradually began to abandon churches and close sites. The introduction of new legislation to protect important medieval ecclesiastical remains was paradoxically the result of many years agitation by the Catholic community. The Irish Church Act of 1869 set out to reduce the number of cathedrals to eight and all other churches would have parish status. The Church of Ireland was disestablished and partially disendowed. The churches which were still in use were vested in the Representative Church Body (RCB). A number of the residual churches, not in use but considered important on the grounds of age or architectural merit, were vested pursuant to Section 25 of the act in the Commissioners of Public Works. The category of National Monument was devised for these buildings. Until this time, the Office of Public Works had been concerned with drainage and other State-sponsored civil engineering works. One of the specific provisions of the document was that the churches could not be used for worship but would be preserved as ruins. The first building to be vested in the Board was the Rock of Cashel in 1873. Before it was fully transferred, a bill was presented in the House of Lords seeking to amend Section 25 of the act so that the Rock of Cashel could be vested in a group of trustees in order that they might restore the cathedral for use by the Catholic Church. The bill was defeated on each occasion. In the case of Holycross Abbey, which is a national monument, when the church was restored for use as a Catholic church a special Act of the Dáil was passed in order to circumvent the original act. The Irish Church Act can be seen as a recognition of antiquarian values, but the effect was to neutralise the danger of their repossession. The exclusion of buildings regularly for use for worship from legal protection carried through to the National Monuments Acts of 1930, and still exists today.

Many of the churches, such as St John's in Kilkenny, St Mary's in New Ross and Thomastown, are the responsibility of two organisations: the Representative Church Body and Dúchas, the Heritage Service. If a church is used for worship it is effectively outside the provisions of the National Monuments Acts. A further complication arises if a section of a church ceases to be used for regular worship, such as the north transept at St Laserian's. It is not clear in this case if it comes under the provisions of the National Monuments Acts, or if the exclusion covers the entire building complex. A recent development is the Conservation Plan, which takes into account the significance of the site and recognises the value of the later interventions. The plan addresses the conservation issues on each individual site and includes all relevant drawings, research and historic data. It includes a record of all church monuments, furniture and fittings, as well as all conservation work carried out at the site. The obligation to making the plan should rest with the bodies responsible for the up-keep of the building. Any proposed alterations to the building fabric is considered in the context of its impact on the building as a whole and only if the management plan has been prepared.

From the antiquarian viewpoint, when seen in isolation the churches are compromised monuments. Unlike St Canice's cathedral for instance, they do not retain their original medieval character. The churches are reduced and partly demolished, but are also rich in information about the society that made them and events in our past. The aspiration of conservation work must be to retain the fabric from all the significant phases of the building's existence. Each phase embodies evidence that has a unique Irish context and importance. The churches are a shared but contested heritage for all the community. Their survival, in this compromised condition, provides physical evidence which illuminates our understanding of the past.

———

ENDNOTES

[1]   Rev W. Carrigan, *The History and Antiquities of the Diocese of Ossory* (Dublin 1905) 297.
[2]   H.G. Leask, *Irish Churches and Monastic Buildings*, 3 vols (Dundalk 1966) iii, 84.
[3]   Carrigan, *History and Antiquities*, 297.
[4]   Rev J.B. Leslie, *Ossory Clergy and Parishes* (Enniskillen 1933) 212.
[5]   *ibid.*, 217
[6]   *ibid.*
[7]   National Monuments file, Dúchas, the Heritage Service (Dublin) F94/732/2, 23.
[8]   *ibid.*, 63.
[9]   Carrigan, *History and Antiquities*, 400.

[10] A. Thomas, *The walled towns of Ireland*, 2 vols (Dublin 1992) i, 115.

[11] A. Gywnn and R.N. Hadcock, *Medieval religious houses in Ireland* (Dublin 1970) 329-30.

[12] Leslie, *Ossory Clergy and Parishes*, 272.

[13] Carrigan, *History and Antiquities*, 90.

[14] *ibid.*

[15] Leslie, *Ossory Clergy and Parishes*, 356.

[16] Carrigan, *History and Antiquities*, 91.

[17] *Journal of the Royal Society of Antiquaries of Ireland*, 1872, 219.

[18] Leslie, *Ossory Clergy and Parishes*, 356.

[19] Carrigan, *History and Antiquities*, 91.

[20] *ibid.*

[21] Thomas, *The walled towns of Ireland*, 179.

[22] Leslie, *Ossory Clergy and Parishes*, 227-8.

[23] P.H. Hore, *History of the Town and County of Wexford* (London 1900) 193.

[24] Leslie, *Ossory Clergy and Parishes*, 228.

[25] *Fourth Report of the Ecclesiastical Commissioners (Ireland)* (London 1833).

[26] Hore, *History of the Town and County of Wexford* (London 1900) 92.

[27] Leask, *Irish Churches and Monastic Buildings*, ii, 117.

[28] Leslie, *Ossory Clergy and Parishes*, 367.

[29] S. Lewis, *A Topographical Dictionary of Ireland* (London 1837) 622.

[30] A Gwyn and R.N. Hadcock, *Medieval religious houses, Ireland* (Dublin 1970) 89.

[31] Sir A. Clapham, *The Archaeological Journal*, memorial supplement (London 1952) 26.

[32] Gwyn and Hadcock, *Medieval religious houses*, 89.

[33] Clapham, *The Archaeological Journal*, memorial supplement, 27.

[34] Gwyn and Hadcock, *Medieval religious houses*, 90.

[35] Carrigan, *History and Antiquities*, 105.

[36] Gwynn and Hadcock, *Medieval religious houses*, 180.

[37] C. Manning, 'The Inistioge Priory Cloister Arcade', *The Old Kilkenny Review*, vol. 1, no. 3, 1976.

[38] Gwynn and Hadcock, *Medieval religious houses*, 180.

[39] *Fourth Report of the Ecclesiastical Commissioners*.

[40] From Richard Langrishe, 'The Priory of Inistioge', *Journal of the Royal Society of Antiquaries of Ireland*, 1874.

[41] Carrigan, *History and Antiquities*, 253.

[42] *ibid.*

[43] *ibid.*

[44] Leslie, *Ossory Clergy and Parishes*, 351.

[45] Carrigan, *History and Antiquities*, 254.

[46] Leslie, *Ossory Clergy and Parishes*, 351.

[47] *ibid.*

[48] *ibid.*

[49] J. Robertson, 'Architectural remains of the Priory of St John, Kilkenny', *Journal of the Royal Society of Antiquaries of Ireland*, vol 1, 1849-51, 433.

[50] *ibid.*, 434.

[51] *Fourth Report of the Ecclesiastical Commissioners*.

[52]   Robertson, 'Architectural remains of the Priory of St John, Kilkenny', 434.

[53]   A. Thomas, *The Walled towns of Ireland* (Dublin 1992) 212.

[54]   Gwynn and Hadcock, *Medieval religious houses*, 198.

[55]   National Monuments File, Dúchas, the Heritage Service (Dublin) F94/680/1.

[56]   M Craig, 'John Semple and his Churches', *Irish Arts Review, 1989-90* (Dublin 1989), 145-6.

[57]   G. Flood, *The History of the Diocese of Ferns* (1915) 142

[58]   National Monuments File, Dúchas, the Heritage Service (Dublin) F94/680/1.

[59]   R. Stalley, *The Cistercian Monasteries of Ireland* (London and New Haven 1987) 72.

[60]   Leask, *Irish Churches and Monastic Buildings*, ii, 86.

[61]   Gwynn and Hadcock, *Medieval religious houses*, 133-4.

[62]   E.W. Hughes, 'Graiguenamanagh', *The Old Kilkenny Review* (1962) 46-7.

[63]   E.W. Hughes, 'Duiske Abbey, Graiguenamanagh', *The Old Kilkenny Review* (1974) 4-5.

[64]   Stalley, *The Cistercian Monasteries of Ireland*, 227.

[65]   S. Swayne, *Duiske Abbey, Graiguenamanagh*, (nd) 6.

[66]   *ibid.*

[67]   *ibid.*

[68]   Hughes, 'Graiguenamanagh', 46-7

[69]   Swayne, *Duiske Abbey, Graiguenamanagh*, 7.

[70]   Hughes, 'Duiske Abbey, Graiguenamanagh', and 'Abbey Triumphant', *The Old Kilkenny Review* (1977) 255-6.

[71]   P. Harbison, *Guide to the National Monumnets in the Republic of Ireland* (Dublin 1970) 340.

[72]   Gwynn and Hadcock, *Medieval religious houses*, 127-8.

[73]   S. Lewis, *A Topographical Dictionary of Ireland*, 101

[74]   Stalley, *The Cistercian Monasteries of Ireland*, 242.

[75]   H. Fenning, *The Black Abbey: The Kilkenny Dominicans, 1225-1996* (nd) 8-9

[76]   Carrigan, *History and Antiquities*, 178.

[77]   N. McCullough and V. Mulvin, *A Lost Tradition – The Nature of Architecture in Ireland* (Dublin 1987) 31.

[78]   Carrigan, *History and Antiquities*, 178.

[79]   Fenning, *The Black Abbey*, 14.

[80]   *ibid.*, 21.

[81]   *ibid.*

---

overleaf

36 – Plans of the case-study churches and St Canice's Cathedral (pp 152-153)

37 – Plans of the case-study churches showing early nineteenth-century alterations (pp 154-155)

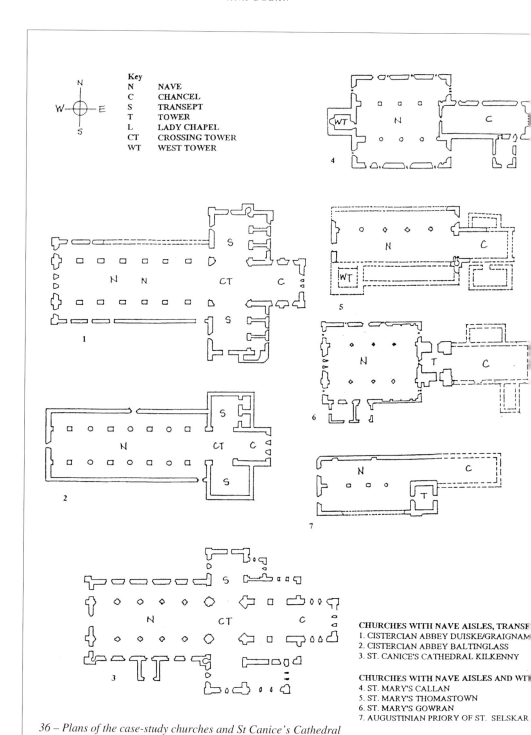

Key
N   NAVE
C   CHANCEL
S   TRANSEPT
T   TOWER
L   LADY CHAPEL
CT   CROSSING TOWER
WT   WEST TOWER

36 – Plans of the case-study churches and St Canice's Cathedral

CHURCHES WITH NAVE AISLES, TRANSE[
1. CISTERCIAN ABBEY DUISKE/GRAIGNAM
2. CISTERCIAN ABBEY BALTINGLASS
3. ST. CANICE'S CATHEDRAL KILKENNY

CHURCHES WITH NAVE AISLES AND WT[
4. ST. MARY'S CALLAN
5. ST. MARY'S THOMASTOWN
6. ST. MARY'S GOWRAN
7. AUGUSTINIAN PRIORY OF ST. SELSKAR

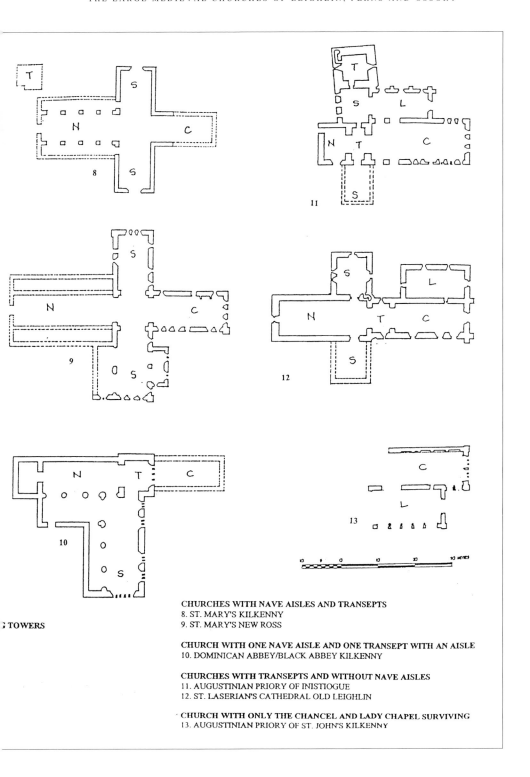

CHURCHES WITH NAVE AISLES AND TRANSEPTS
8. ST. MARY'S KILKENNY
9. ST. MARY'S NEW ROSS

CHURCH WITH ONE NAVE AISLE AND ONE TRANSEPT WITH AN AISLE
10. DOMINICAN ABBEY/BLACK ABBEY KILKENNY

CHURCHES WITH TRANSEPTS AND WITHOUT NAVE AISLES
11. AUGUSTINIAN PRIORY OF INISTIOGUE
12. ST. LASERIAN'S CATHEDRAL OLD LEIGHLIN

CHURCH WITH ONLY THE CHANCEL AND LADY CHAPEL SURVIVING
13. AUGUSTINIAN PRIORY OF ST. JOHN'S KILKENNY

153

*37 – Plans of the case-study churches
showing early nineteenth-century alterations*

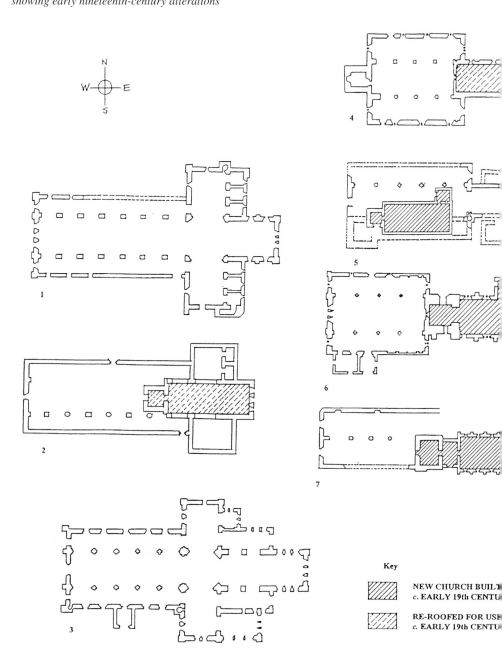

Key

NEW CHURCH BUILT
c. EARLY 19th CENTU

RE-ROOFED FOR USE
c. EARLY 19th CENTU

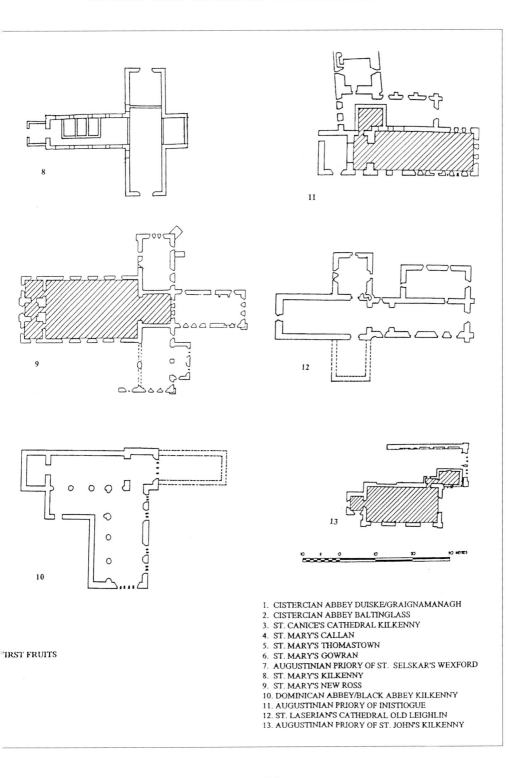

FIRST FRUITS

1. CISTERCIAN ABBEY DUISKE/GRAIGNAMANAGH
2. CISTERCIAN ABBEY BALTINGLASS
3. ST. CANICE'S CATHEDRAL KILKENNY
4. ST. MARY'S CALLAN
5. ST. MARY'S THOMASTOWN
6. ST. MARY'S GOWRAN
7. AUGUSTINIAN PRIORY OF ST. SELSKAR'S WEXFORD
8. ST. MARY'S KILKENNY
9. ST. MARY'S NEW ROSS
10. DOMINICAN ABBEY/BLACK ABBEY KILKENNY
11. AUGUSTINIAN PRIORY OF INISTIOGUE
12. ST. LASERIAN'S CATHEDRAL OLD LEIGHLIN
13. AUGUSTINIAN PRIORY OF ST. JOHN'S KILKENNY

Shanganagh Castle, Co Dublin
the Entrance Hall, looking to the front door (all photographs courtesy Mrs Barbara Clarke)

Shanganagh Castle and
the bottle letter

PETER PEARSON

O N THE SHORES OF KILLINEY BAY, SITUATED IN THE SUBURBS OF DUBLIN, LIES Shanganagh Castle, a late-Georgian house built in the picturesque battle-mented Gothic style. The castle, which is now an open prison managed by the Department of Justice, may be found just halfway between Shankill and Bray, on the old main road (also the old coach road) to Wexford.

It would appear that a plain bow-ended house was erected near the ruins of the old castle sometime during the 1790s, at a time when south Co Dublin was becoming a popular place of residence. Between the years 1805 and 1818 the house was completely remodelled by Sir George Cockburn, and the ruined tower or castle was dismantled. Cockburn tells us, in the 'bottle letter' discussed below, that the stones from this tower were used to build the chimney and tower of his picture gallery in the new house. He also mentions that some cannon shot was found in the rubble.

Cockburn, who, it would appear, was very wealthy, left an eleven-page man-uscript for posterity enclosed in a bottle and buried in a wall in the castle. The letter was discovered by workmen in 1954, when the Office of Public Works were making alterations. The letter is of great interest not only because it gives a date and a description of the work which he carried out, but also because he gives us his views on the politics of the day and his thoughts on religion.

The letter was written by a man who had assembled an impressive collection of antiquities, sculpture, painting and armoury during his extensive travels in Europe, where he had witnessed the effects of the Napoleonic wars. His collection remained at Shanganagh Castle until the 1920s, when it was sold by public auction by his descendants. A number of photographs of the castle and its collection are included in this article, courtesy of Barbara Clarke, whose family, the Wentworth-Allens, once lived there. This unique collection of photographs was taken in the early 1900s, and shows how magnificently furnished the castle was.

The castle is entered through an elegant, pillared hallway. The principal

Shanganagh Castle, Co Dublin

*1 – Additions and alterations by
Richard Morrison from c.1803
and after, including the bow-ended
late eighteenth-century house to
the rear*

*2 – The Entrance Hall, looking
from the front door*

opposite

4 – The Picture Gallery

5 – The Music Room

rooms are decorated in the neo-classical style – the largest being the shallow-vault-ed picture gallery – and many are provided with niches which once held items from his remarkable collection of classical sculptures. Cockburn's new work was carried out under the direction of Richard Morrison, and the contemporary accounts and papers of Bryan Bolger record two visits to the castle. These include one in 1805 to take measurements for the rebuilding.[1] The sculpture gallery referred to in the latter was accommodated in the north wing, and was given particular notice by Brewer in his *Beauties of Ireland*, who referred to 'Antique Bronzes, mosaic and Egyptian granite tables', and 'numerous volcanic specimens from Mounts Vesuvius and Aetna'.[2] Cockburn was a contemporary of the architect and collector Sir John Soane in London, whose own remarkable collection is still displayed to the public in his purpose-built home-museum.

Cockburn's bottle letter begins by describing in some depth the positions of the various ruined castles between Shankill and Bray, and ends with a remarkable castigation of contemporary politics and religion. Fortunately his anticipation of the 'finale' of Shanganagh Castle itself, inspired by his thoughts on transience and the passage of time, have not been realised to date. While the sculpture gallery has been dismantled and the exterior has been simplified, the house remains well kept by the Department of Justice, and many of Cockburn's plastercasts and sculptures are still to be seen, especially in the walls of the hall and staircase.

––––––

COPY OF DOCUMENT FOUND IN A BOTTLE AT SHANGANAGH CASTLE DURING BUILDING OPERATIONS BY THE OFFICE OF PUBLIC WORKS IN 1954

The bottle the... Enclosed in wall 1st July 1818.
1818 Second of May

I, G Cockburn commenced the alteration and addition to my house.

There was an old Tower here, but in a very ruinous state, being some of the small remains of the Old Castle. The Tower was badly built, so I took its Remains down, & built this on the site of the former one, both as orna-mental, & as a chimney to my Picture Gallery. In taking it down we found Two Cannon Shot which are replaced at the same height, in which they were in the old Tower: – but how they came there – no one can tell-

There was certainly a Redoubt & Fortification formerly in my North Sea Field – next the Martello Tower – but so much of the sea bank has fallen

6 – Shanganagh Castle
detail of the sculpture collection

in; that very little remains of it at this day – & it has been diminished in my own Memory – There was a Line of Fortification in this part formerly – commencing at Shanganagh Castle – near sea and Leighlings town [Loughlinstown] communicating to Pucks Castle – a strong redoubt and field work on part of Shankill – the remains of which are now visible; and easily traced thence to Ballyman Old Court & ending at Bray, where there is still the remains of an Old Castle. It appears to have formed a sort of Cordon, making a half-circle, or rather oval, from Bray to Leighlings town, the Radius of which from above this spot to Ballyman is at least 2 [?] miles and the Diameter from Bray to Leighlings town 3 miles. There were Castles also along the Coast to Dublin (& some towards Wicklow) at Bulloch, Dalkey and Monks Town – But no records of what time built. This coast was certainly in former times much frequented by Pirates: – & The incursions of the Tooles from the Forests & Woods in the County of Wicklow could only be restrained by Garrisons & Castles. In those rude times however Cannon were so little in use, & particularly with those Barbarians and Rapparees, either by sea or land, that these shot found in the old Tower & now replaced must have been lodged there in more modern times. Possibly during the Civil Wars – in Cromwell's time or afterwards in King William's.

James certainly slept in Bray Castle after the Battle of the Boyne & fled in this direction – of course he must have had friends adherents and Garrisons here & most likely these shot were from some of William's Cruisers, who might be employed to scour the coast. So far for antiquity.

As to modern times I enclose a Newspaper in this Bottle – Whether in our Damp Climate it will be preserved is more than I can tell – I shall be probably long dead and decomposed before this Bottle is disturbed – But like all things on Earth – This Tower and This Bottle will come to their finale – also – Should this be preserved and hereafter found – the Reader may rely on its correctness and wishing the future owners of This House, as much pleasure and enjoyment as I have had in it and as I am at all events the Improver and chief builder of it; I hope they will do me The favour to Drink to my memory a Bumper of Good Claret – if our descendants are allowed to drink of that good liquor. At present the enormous Tax on Wine has nearly put its consumption down.

As to the Politicks – in this Extraordinary Age the Historian will perhaps like to know the secret wishes and opinions of the present day & here it is:-

Altho Napoleon Buonaparte threw away his good fortune, & by attempting to Conquer all the world was himself conquered, & the French

Shanganagh Castle

7 – Garden statue of a grotesque warrior

8 – Ornamental Column

Nation as much degraded & sunk – as it was a few years before exalted – & after a struggle of 25 years – & France having arrived at a pitch of Military Glory never Exceeded; we who are on the stage in this year 1818 – have witnessed her degradation & the shameful apathy with which the Present French (forgetting the glorious exploits of their brethren so lately) – have submitted to have the imbecile and Rascally Bourbons forced on them – Nevertheless – it is a fact that however highly we may admire and rejoice at the success of our own Brave Soldiers – still every fair & honest, & wise unpensioned man deplores the return of the Bourbons & all the Race of Legitimates – but particularly of that cruel ungrateful & ever to be detested Monster – Ferdinand King of Spain. If Mankind relapse into ignorance and Despotism so much the worse for those who are to live hereafter – but if, (as is the opinion of the best informed) in a short time there is a Rally – The thing will be to do over again, & corrupt & profligate as mankind are, the struggle may end in a new compact beneficial to the Human Race.

God Grant it may be so But whether it will be or whether the Races of Kings Lords & Priests will have another century of fine times keeping the People in the Dark or whether the Artful and Designing Russian who has been so foolishly introduced in to Europe, will overrun and conquer it – Establishing Darkness & Despotism – The illustration will more likely be known to the finder of this Bottle.

I am now 54 years of age – my Winter approaches – Should I live to be 80 I shall (I think) see many changes – and whether I do or not – Believe me – gentle reader – I am an honest constitutional man. My Religion is to be honest & just to all men, kind & benevolent to all, but rigid & strict, not overlooking crimes – I believe in a God – I do not believe one word of the terrible humbug story of Christianity; with which so large a portion of Mankind have been so long duped as to the Resurrection of the Body – I doubt it and if it be so – I may know what you are doing 1000 years hence – I shall be no worse than those who went before, & who will go after me.

Vale

Geo. Cockburn.

———

ENDNOTES

1 Edward McParland, Alistair Rowan and Ann Martha Rowan, *The Architecture of Richard Morrison and William Vitruvius Morrison* (Dublin 1989) 159-60.
2 J.N. Brewer, *The Beauties of Ireland*, 2 vols (London 1825-6) i, 273-4.

9 – Shanganagh Castle
monument to the Reform Bill, part of which still stands

A database of Irish architects 1720-1940: E & F

IRISH ARCHITECTURAL ARCHIVE

AT THE IRISH ARCHITECTURAL ARCHIVE IN DUBLIN, A DATABASE OF IRISH architects and their works is being compiled. The project was described in the *Bulletin of the Irish Georgian Society*, xxxvi (1994) 75-77. Since that article was written, inputting has reached the letter O. There has also been a slight contraction of the date range. The rather arbitrary range of 1700-1950 has been changed to 1720-1940. 1720 has been preferred as being the date at which Rolf Loeber's *A biographical dictionary of architects in Ireland 1600-1720* (1981) ends, and 1940 as reflecting the natural break in architectural and building activity in Ireland caused by the Second World War.

The following list is of persons included in the database whose names begin with the letters E and F. It includes some engineers and some builders and craftsmen. The symbol * following the name indicates a builder or craftsman; the symbol # indicates a foreigner – usually English or Scottish – who carried out work in Ireland but was never based in this country. Dates of birth and death are given, when known, followed by the quarter centuries in which the subject is believed to have been active professionally.

ANN MARTHA ROWAN
Irish Architectural Archive

167

name	born / died	flourished
EACRET, Charles *		19c2, 19c3
EAGAR, Thomas Robert	c.1888-c.1974	20c1, 20c2, 20c3
EAGER, William *		18c4
EARL, Peter *		19c2
EARLEY & CO *		20c1, 20c2, 20c3
EARLEY & POWELL *		19c3, 19c4
EARLEY, John Bishop *	c.1856-1935	19c3, 19c4, 20c1
EARLEY, John Farrington *	1831-1873	19c2, 19c3
EARLEY, Thomas *	1819-1893	19c2, 19c3, 19c4
EARLEY, William *	1872-1956	19c4, 20c1, 20c2
EASTON, Alexander #	1787-1854	19c1, 19c2, 19c3
EATON, Benjamin [1]*	d.1798	18c4
EATON, Benjamin [2]*		18c4, 19c1
EATON, Benjamin [3]		19c1, 19c2
EATON, Cosby *	d.c.1816	19c1
EATON, William		19c4
ECCLES, W. #		20c1
EDGAR, Edward *		19c1
EDGAR, Patrick		18c3
EDGEWORTH, David Reid	1842-1871	19c3
EDGEWORTH, Richard Lovell	1744-1817	18c3, 18c4, 19c1
EDGEWORTH, William	1794-1829	19c1, 19c2
EDIS, Robert William (Sir) #	1839-1927	19c3, 19c4, 20c1
EDWARDES, Oswald J. #		20c1
EDWARDS, —	d.1787	18c4
EDWARDS, Kendrick	1875-1943	20c1, 20c2
EDWARDS, Osborne Cadwallader	1822-1876	19c2, 19c3, 19c4
EDWARDS, Thomas	1815-1882	19c2, 19c3, 19c4
EDWIN, Richard #	d.1778	18c3, 18c4
EGAN, James J.	c.1840-1915	19c3, 19c4, 20c1
EGAN, John *		18c3, 18c4
EGAN, Robert *		19c1, 19c2
ELCOCK, Charles Ernest	1878-1944	19c4, 20c1, 20c2
ELDER, Charles *		19c2
ELGEE, William		18c2
ELGIN, —		20c1
ELLIOTT FAMILY *		18c3, 18c4, 19c1

ELLIOTT, Andrew *		19c1, 19c2
ELLIOTT, D.B.		20c2
ELLIOTT, John M.	d.1938	20c1, 20c2
ELLIOTT, Patrick Hugh	d.1937	20c1, 20c2
ELLIOTT, Robert	c.1863-1910	19c4, 20c1
ELLIOTT, Thomas [1]		19c2
ELLIOTT, Thomas [2]	c.1833-1915	19c3, 19c4, 20c1
ELLIS, William H. Mandeville	d.1911	19c4, 20c1
ELMES, James #	1782-1862	19c1, 19c2, 19c3
ELSAM, Richard #		18c4, 19c1
EMDEN, Thomas Walter Lawrence #	1847-1913	19c3, 19c4, 20c1
EMERY, Henry *		19c3, 19c4
ENRIGHT, J.E.		20c1
ENSOR, George	d.1803	18c2, 18c3, 18c4
ENSOR, John	d.1787	18c2, 18c3, 18c4
ENTWHISTLE, James		19c3
ESDALL, George		18c3
ESMONDE, Bartholomew	1789-1862	19c1, 19c2
ESSEX, James #	1722-1784	18c2, 18c3, 18c4
EVANS, Ambrose		18c3
EVANS, James		19c4, 20c1, 20c2
EVANS, John D.		19c4
EVANS, Richard [1]	d.1802	18c4, 19c1
EVANS, Richard [2]		19c3
EVANS, Richard [3]	c.1941	19c4, 20c1, 20c2
EVANS, Robert Edward		20c1, 20c2
EVATT, Humphrey	1839-1865	19c3
EVERARD, — #		18c3
EVERETT, J.E.		20c1
EWART, James		19c3, 19c4
EWING, John		18c4
EYRE, Thomas	d.1772	18c2, 18c3
FAHEY, — *		19c3
FAHIE, J. Angelo		19c4
FAHIE, James Keyes	1809-1899	19c2, 19c3, 19c4
FAHY, Owen		19c1, 19c2
FAHY, Richard		19c1
FAIR, J.R.		20c1

name	born / died	flourished
FAIRBAIRN, William & Son #		19c3
FAIRBURN, William #		18c4
FAIRCLOTH, William *		19c3
FAIRWEATHER, John Matthew	1882-1961	20c1, 20c2, 20c3
FALKNER, John *		18c2
FANT, James		20c1
FARIS, Richard		19c2
FARIS, Robert	--	19c2
FARQUHARSON, Horace Cowley Nesham #	1875-1966	19c4, 20c1, 20c2
FARRALL, James Joseph	d.1911	19c4, 20c1
FARRANGE		18c2
FARRELL & SON *		19c2, 19c3, 19c4
FARRELL & SONS *		19c2, 19c3, 19c4
FARRELL, Edward [1]		19c1
FARRELL, Edward [2]		19c1
FARRELL, Edward [3]*		19c2
FARRELL, Francis James		19c2, 19c3
FARRELL, George *		19c1, 19c2, 19c3
FARRELL, Isaac		19c2, 19c3
FARRELL, James		18c4
FARRELL, James Barry	1810-1893	19c2, 19c3, 19c4
FARRELL, John [1]*		18c4, 19c1
FARRELL, John [2]*		19c1
FARRELL, John [3]*		19c2
FARRELL, John [4]*		19c2
FARRELL, Martin John		19c3
FARRELL, Patrick [1]		18c4
FARRELL, Patrick [2]		19c1
FARRELL, Patrick [3]*		19c1
FARRELL, Patrick [4]*		19c1
FARRELL, Patrick [5]*		19c2
FARRELL, Patrick [6]*		19c2
FARRELL, Peter *		19c1
FARRELL, Philip *		19c2
FARRELL, William	d.1851	19c1, 19c2, 19c3
FARRELL, William Robert		19c3

FARRINGTON, Stephen W.	*c.*1889-1965	20c1, 20c2, 20c3
FAULKNER, Edward *		19c2
FAULKNER, Samuel	d.1795	18c3, 18c4
FAWCETT, James *		18c4
FAWCETT, William Milner #	1832-1908	19c3, 19c4, 20c1
FEEHAN, Malachi A.		20c1, 20c2, 20c3
FELL, Richard *		19c2
FELL, William *		19c1
FELLOW, John #		18c3
FENNELL & CLARKE		20c1
FENNELL, William Bertram	d.1938	19c4, 20c1, 20c2
FENNELL, William John	d.1923	19c4, 20c1
FERGUSON & McILVEEN		20c1, 20c2, 20c3
FERGUSON, Acheson C.	*c.*1849-1938	19c4, 20c1, 20c2
FERGUSON, Duncan C.		19c2, 19c3
FERGUSON, George & Robert A. *		19c3
FERGUSON, Godfrey William	*c.*1859-1939	19c4, 20c1, 20c2
FERGUSON, James		19c4, 20c1
FERGUSON, James R.A.		19c4, 20c1
FERGUSON, John [1]		18c4, 19c1
FERGUSON, John [2]		19c2
FERGUSON, John Guy	d.1901	19c3, 19c4
FERGUSON, Matthew		19c1
FERGUSON, Robert	1887-1981	20c1, 20c2, 20c3
FERGUSON, Robert A.		19c3, 19c4
FERNSLEY, James		18c3, 18c4, 19c1
FERREY, Benjamin #	1810-1880	19c2, 19c3, 19c4
FETHERSTON, Edward		19c2
FETHERSTON, William		19c2
FETHERSTONE, —		19c3
FFORDE, Francis Creswell	d.1949	20c1, 20c2
FIDLER, Thomas Claxton		19c4
FIELD, Booth (or Boyle)		18c4, 19c1
FIELDING, James *		19c1, 19c2
FIELDSEND, —		19c4
FIGGIS, Thomas Phillips	1858-1948	19c4, 20c1, 20c2
FINNERAN, Francis		19c2
FITZ-GIBBON, Abraham Coates	1823-1887	19c2, 19c3, 18c4
FITZGERALD, —		19c1

name	born / died	flourished
FITZGERALD, Edward (Sir)*	b.1846	19c3, 19c4, 20c1
FITZGERALD, Edward [1]*		19c1, 19c2
FITZGERALD, Edward [2]	1820-1893	19c2, 19c3, 19c4
FITZGERALD, Gerald (Lord)	b.1821	19c2, 19c3
FITZGERALD, Laurence McO'Boy		19c3, 19c4, 20c1
FITZGERALD, M.		19c4
FITZGERALD, Maurice [1]*		18c4
FITZGERALD, Maurice [2]		19c3
FITZGERALD, Maurice [3]		19c4
FITZGERALD, Maurice [4]		20c1
FITZGERALD, Michael		19c1, 19c2
FITZGERALD, Michael F.		19c1
FITZGERALD, Thomas [1]		19c2
FITZGERALD, Thomas [2]		19c3, 19c4
FITZGIBBON, Anthony		20c2
FITZHENRY, — *		19c2
FITZMAURICE, Maurice	1861-1924	19c4, 20c1
FITZPATRICK & MOLLOY *		19c3, 19c4
FITZPATRICK, Anthony *		19c1
FITZPATRICK, Daniel *		19c1, 19c2
FITZPATRICK, Denis *	c.1768-1813	18c4
FITZPATRICK, John [1]*		19c1
FITZPATRICK, John [2]*		19c1, 19c2
FITZPATRICK, Thomas *		19c3
FITZPATRICK, William		19c1
FITZSIMMONS, J.J.		20c2
FITZSIMMONS, Maurice		20c1
FITZSIMONS, J.F.		20c1
FITZSIMONS, James A.M		20c1, 20c2
FITZSIMONS, Nicholas	1869-c.1940	19c4, 20c1, 20c2
FITZSIMONS, Patrick *		19c2
FITZSIMONS, Thomas		18c3
FLACK, Charles Horatio #		19c4, 20c1
FLAHERTY, Edmund *		18c3, 18c4
FLAHERTY, William *	d.1800	18c4
FLANAGAN, —		19c4
FLANAGAN, James H.	d.c.1946	20c2

FLANAGAN, Thomas		19c1
FLANAGAN, Thomas Patrick		20c1, 20c2, 20c3
FLANAGIN, Hugh William		20c1, 20c2
FLANIGAN, John Gerald		20c1
FLANNIGEN, John *		18c3
FLEMING, George H.		20c1, 20c2
FLEMING, J.P.		20c1
FLEMING, John Joseph		20c1
FLEMING, M.J.	c.1843-1910	19c4, 20c1
FLEMING, N. *		19c2
FLETCHER, William *	d.1818	19c1
FLEURY, Christopher *		19c2
FLINN, Michael *		19c2
FLINN, Nicholas *		19c2
FLOOD, H.		20c2
FLOWER, Lamorock #		19c3
FOGARTH, John *		19c1
FOGARTY, E.		20c1
FOGARTY, Gerard P.	d.1965	20c1, 20c2, 20c3
FOGARTY, John	1907-1962	20c2, 20c3
FOGARTY, Lawrence *		19c2
FOGERTY, John [1]*		19c1
FOGERTY, John [2]		19c2, 19c3
FOGERTY, John Frederick	1863-1938	19c4, 20c1, 20c2
FOGERTY, John & Son		19c3
FOGERTY, Joseph [1]	d.1887	19c2, 19c3, 19c4
FOGERTY, Joseph [2]	1831-1899	19c3, 19c4
FOGERTY, Joseph [3]		20c1
FOGERTY, Joseph & Son		19c4, 20c1
FOGERTY, Robert	c.1843-1907	19c3, 19c4, 20c1
FOGERTY, William	c.1833-1878	19c3, 19c4
FOLEY & O'sULLIVAN		20c1, 20c2
FOLEY, John		19c2
FOLEY, John Henry *	1818-1874	19c2, 19c3
FOLEY, Patrick J.		20c1, 20c2
FOLEY, Peter *		19c2
FOLEY, Thomas *		19c2
FOOT, Edward		18c3
FOOT, F.R.		19c4

name	born / died	flourished
FORBES, J.R.		20c2
FORBES, John Robinson		20c2, 20c3
FORBES, R.B.	c.1854-1909	19c4, 20c1
FORBES, Robert Edwin		20c1, 20c2
FORDE, Arthur William	1821-1886	19c2, 19c3, 19c4
FORDE, G.		19c1
FORDE, Henry Charles	1827-1897	19c2, 19c3, 19c4
FORESTER, John		18c4
FORMAN & ASTON		19c4
FORMAN, Alfred A.		19c4, 20c1
FORREST, Edward		19c2
FORSETT, —		18c4
FORSYTH, Thomas		19c4, 20c1
FORSYTH, W.		18c4
FORSYTH, William [1]		18c4
FORSYTH, William [2]		19c2, 19c3, 19c4
FORSYTH, William Adam #	1872-1951	19c4, 20c1, 20c2
FORSYTHE, R.G.	d.1934	20c2
FORTE, Felix		20c2, 20c3, 20c4
FORTESCUE, George Alan #		20c1, 20c2
FORTESCUE, Matthew		19c4, 20c1
FORTH, Charles Gerard	d.1846	19c2
FOSBERY, Thomas		19c3, 19c4
FOSTER, F.W. #		20c1
FOSTER, H. #		20c1
FOTTRELL, John		19c4
FOULSTON, John #	1772-1841	18c4, 19c1, 19c2
FOWKE, Francis	1823-1865	19c2, 19c3
FOWLER, E.		19c3
FOWLER, John (Sir) #	1817-1899	19c2, 19c3, 19c4
FOWLER, Richard #		19c1
FOWLER, William	d.1796	18c4
FOY, Henry Bertram	1893-1932	20c1, 20c2
FOY, Patrick or Peter *		19c3
FRALY, Andrew *		19c1
FRAMPTON, Edward #*		19c4
FRANKLIN, Anthony		18c4

FRANKLIN, Frederick	1828-1905	19c2, 19c3, 19c4
FRASER, James	1793-1863	19c1, 19c2, 19c3
FRASER, John	d.1874	19c2, 19c3
FRASER, John, & Son(s)		19c4, 20c1
FRASER, Samuel Gordon	b.1845	19c3, 19c4, 20c1
FRASER, William		19c2
FRATER, Robert	d.1957	20c1, 20c2, 20c3
FRAZER, FERGUSON & FRAZER		19c3
FRAZER, Thomas		19c1
FREEMAN, Daniel J.	d.1902	19c3, 19c4
FREEMAN, Joseph Kelly		19c4, 20c1
FREEMAN, Richard Knill #	1838/9-1904	19c3, 19c4, 20c1
FREEMAN, SON & GASKILL #		20c1
FRENCH, John *		19c2
FRENCH, Richard		18c3
FREND, William Arthur	1858-1889	19c4
FRIEL, William	c.1874-1970	19c4, 20c1, 20c2
FRITH, John Henry		19c2
FRITH, Richard Hastings	c.1815-1873	19c2, 19c3
FRITH, William		19c2
FROST & CLOTWORTHY #		20c1
FULLER & JERMYN		20c1, 20c2
FULLER, James Franklin	1835-1925	19c3, 19c4, 20c1
FULLERTON, John Henry		19c3, 19c4, 20c1
FULLERTON, William	d.1866/67	19c3
FULTON, H.T.		19c4
FULTON, Henry	1793-1859	19c1, 19c2, 19c3
FURNACE, John		18c3

———

Shorter Notices

1 – Skidmore Owings & Merrill's proposal for George's Quay, Dublin,
opposite Gandon's Custom House and on the peripheral boundary of Trinity College

A greedy Celtic tiger

MARY BRYAN

FROM A CONSERVATION POINT OF VIEW, THE CELTIC TIGER IS A TWO-FACED ANImal. Prosperity means that there is a lot more money around and more restoration work being carried out by public and private bodies, as well as by individuals. In the private sector, firms are sponsoring restoration projects, and many period houses in varying stages of neglect are being purchased and, in many cases, lovingly restored by the owners. The restoration and refurbishment carried out on Dublin's eighteenth-century City Hall by Dublin Corporation is a case in point. This major building has, for many years, languished in shabbiness and with inappropriate interventions, but now its inherent qualities and interior splendour are once again revealed.

This type of restoration would have been inconceivable not so very long ago. Compared with ten years ago, the conservation scene has changed radically in Ireland, with a heightened awareness of the need to care for the built heritage and environment. This new and welcome attitude is evident from government and local authority level through to house owners and the general public. The government has put legislation and funding in place which will greatly strengthen the protection of the heritage. This includes a new survey to extend listing and laws extending protection to curtilage buildings.

But there is a less benevolent side to the rampant creature. Land values have soared so every piece of land becomes an object of desire (greed?), and the historic building on or adjacent to this land is viewed as being of little or no importance when factored into the profit margins of the developers. Planning applications are being made every day to demolish good, solid Georgian, Victorian and Edwardian houses (which have slipped through the net of the Protected Buildings listing) standing in their own grounds in order to cover the site with apartment blocks to the highest possible density. Rarely is the opportunity used to make the existing house the centrepiece of the new development; profit motives override all other considerations.

The dearth of experienced architects, joiners, stonecutters, users of lime-based mortars, etc, has been exacerbated by the fast pace generated by the economic boom and the current hugely increased interest in restoration. Realising the shortage some years ago, the Irish Georgian Society, compiled *Traditional Building and Conservation Skills – Register of Practitioners, 1998.* The updated edition (2000) has just been published with a 50% increase in the number of entries.

Much work is being done by various government and educational bodies to put training structures for traditional skills in place, and a whole new area of employment has been opened up. Each year the Irish Georgian Society runs a two-day exhibition of traditional building skills, and in excess of 5,000 people pour through over the weekend, seeking information and seeing that these skills are alive and well and in need of trainees.

The infill of back gardens of protected structures is another area where many a battle is fought between developers and conservation. Recently enacted legislation will help to modify this particular threat. In rural areas there is unbridled building as well, with apparently little or no checks or consideration for historic streetscapes, landscapes or coastal amenities. A little town in Co Leitrim has just had half a mile of its precious tiny stretch of shoreline covered with houses, and with more to come. This type of random development, which is not governed by an overall policy, is destroying the countryside.

On a larger scale, the escalation of demand for high-rise office/residential blocks has caused some major planning confrontations. Dublin is essentially a low-rise city, and this is a fundamental element defining its character (and attraction to tourists). Its non-threatening, low-rise ambience is one of its greatest assets, together with its important eighteenth-century civic buildings, Trinity College, and its Georgian core encircled by a Victorian band of mainly residential-type architecture. So when, in 1999, planning permission for a group of buildings, the highest to be 73 metres, was applied for in the city centre, the battle was on. The buildings themselves, designed by Skidmore Owings & Merrill, were innovative and well regarded from an architectural point of view (Plate 1). It was the location – on George's Quay, opposite Gandon's Custom House and on the peripheral boundary of Trinity College – that was worrying conservationists. The scheme was eventually refused on appeal, as was the subsequent 500,000 square metre mini-Manhattan up to 90 metres high proposed for further down the Liffey at Spencer Dock (Plate 2).

These 'battles' to protect Dublin's historic core indicate the problems (from a conservation point of view) of an expanding city which requires more offices and more housing. Other cities outside Ireland have, of course, had similar problems, but the height, bulk and sheer size of these proposals was a first for Dublin – the outcome of increased prosperity. A city must evolve, but the pace of developing

*2 – Part of Roche Dinkeloo's proposals for Spencer Dock, Dublin,
a mini-Manhattan on the Liffey, with office blocks up to 90 metres high*

Dublin has caught everyone unprepared.

It is not only urban areas. Another huge area of concern, which is the result of prosperity on an unprecedented scale, is the upgrading of roads and the building of bypasses all over the country. With European money to be spent, usually to a deadline, there have been ill-conceived options proposed for many of these roads. In producing viable options (from its point of view), the road design office in Waterford proposed to demolish the gatelodge at eighteenth-century Whitfield Court and go through a protected habitat of bogland and parkland. Another option would slice through the shelter belts of the park and outstanding gardens at the major estate of Mount Congreve. This renowned collection of flowers, shrubs and trees would be severely damaged by the loss of its shelter belts.

The proposed Mitchelstown bypass and Mitchelstown Traffic Management Programme would have many damaging implications for the unique eighteenth-century set piece of Kingston College in Mitchelstown, Co Cork. This major square, of national importance, has just been granted millions for restoration in State and EU funding. One of the proposed routes for the Navan town bypass goes right through the parkland and driveways of Ardbraccan House – a historic eighteenth-century house of national importance, being carefully restored at great expense by the current owners. St Ultan's Well and the Sacred Oaks are among the wealth of ancient historic sites in this parkland; these would be lost if this route were to be implemented.

Some of these options appear to have been dropped after lengthy objections. The Irish Georgian Society has asked again and again for road design offices to have a proper conservation input. Only when a route is chosen is consideration given to an Environmental Impact Statement (EIS). One is tempted to the cynical conclusion that large estates are chosen for some road options so that only one owner needs to be dealt with instead of numerous small property owners.

A spin-off of this infrastructural work is the need for the materials to construct roads, resulting in historic houses and landscapes being damaged by permission to operate quarries. Kilree House, Bennettsbridge, Co Kilkenny is an example. A nearby quarry has been operating for some time although it fails to comply with the conditions of permission. Now further permission has been granted for, among other things, a fourfold increase in production, an asphalt plant and a 35 metre-high smoke stack. All this at the heart of an area whose scenic and tourist activity has led to the village of Bennettsbridge being included in an EU-sponsored pilot programme on identification of potential scenic parks.

Conservationists are well aware that everything cannot be saved. The country and its cities must expand and evolve. More housing is needed, more office accommodation is needed, and more roads are needed. Everywhere is bursting at the seams, but ad hoc, random development, a lot of it to mediocre standards, is not the way to deal with the situation. Unless a halt is called to ill-prepared planning schemes, our heritage will be irrevocably damaged.

Huge low-density suburbs are being rolled out, yet there a thousands of empty homes above shops. Ireland is not alone in having the problems which this situation creates, such as lack of life in the streets outside of working hours, deterioration of the building fabric, and vandalism. A scheme was launched some years ago to encourage people to live over shops, but it was not a success; living in the city did not prove to be an attractive option. A similar scheme is now being launched in five cities in Ireland by the Department of the Environment and Local Government. So much has the scene changed that there are high expectations of success, but it is in a worrying overall context. Poverty and neglect over many years has saved much of our heritage; prosperity in a few short years looks likely to decimate it. This is in spite of vastly improved legislation, the establishment on a statutory basis of the Heritage Council, and a genuine general wish to look after our heritage for the next generation. All parties involved in these exciting times, including conservationists, should stand back, take stock, co-operate, and work out overall policies and strategies.

Irish people bemoan the many historic buildings lost or damaged in the 'sixties by ill-conceived development, and wonder how such wholesale destruction could have happened. If we are not careful, future generations will look aghast at current development and ask in wonder and horror: 'What were they thinking of at the turn of the century?'

———

ENDNOTES

This article first appeared in the London-published *Building Design*'s Ireland supplement in October 2000.

ILLUSTRATIONS

Illustrations taken from Frank McDonald's *The Construction of Dublin* (Gandon Editions, Kinsale, 2000)

Desmond Guinness Scholarship

THE DESMOND GUINNESS SCHOLARSHIP WILL BE awarded annually by the Irish Georgian Foundation to an applicant or applicants resident in Ireland engaged in research on the visual arts in Ireland, or on the work of Irish architects, artists and craftsmen at home and abroad from 1600 to 1900. Special emphasis will be placed on work based on original documentary research. The total value of the scholarship fund available for distribution in any year is in the region of one thousand pounds.

Forms are available from:

IRISH GEORGIAN SOCIETY
74 Merrion Square
Dublin 2

tel: 01-6767073
fax: 01-6620290
e-mail: igs@iol.ie

Irish Georgian Society

CONSERVING IRELAND'S ARCHITECTURAL HERITAGE

THE IRISH GEORGIAN SOCIETY AIMS TO ENCOURAGE AN INTEREST IN AND TO promote the preservation of distinguished examples of architecture and the allied arts in Ireland. These aims are achieved by:

- MEMBERSHIP – The Society has 3,000 members worldwide. Its headquarters are in Dublin, and there is a thriving and long-established London Chapter and two local Irish chapters in Birr and Limerick. The headquarters of the US membership, IGS Inc., is in New York, and there are local chapters in Boston, Chicago, Cleveland, Columbus, Washington, Minneapolis and Atlanta. The benefits of membership include: (i) a twice-yearly newsletter which includes the events programme; (ii) the annual journal; (iii) free entry to selected historic houses in Ireland.

- FUNDRAISING – The Society runs an events programme which includes: (i) lectures, (ii) private theatre evenings, (iii) architectural walking tours, (iv) conferences and seminars, (v) day tours, including visits to houses not normally open to the public, and (vi) tours abroad.

- EDUCATION – The Society's annual journal, which has been published regularly since 1958, contains articles of original research, and is the only Irish periodical devoted entirely to the architectural history of Ireland. In addition, valuable research in the field of conservation is funded by the Desmond Guinness Scholarship.

- GRANTS – Donations to the Society and funds raised through the events programme enable the Society to make grants towards the restoration of historic properties.

- PLANNING PARTICIPATION – The Society takes an active part in the planning process on a country-wide basis, and opposes planning applications which are not compatible with the principles of good conservation. It also provides general advice on other aspects of conservation.

The Society liaises with government departments in the area of conservation. The Government has accepted that the preservation and conservation of Ireland's historic buildings, precincts, properties and collections should be given high priority.

HISTORY

The Irish Georgian Society was founded in 1958 by the Hon Desmond Guinness and his late wife, Mariga, for the protection of buildings of architectural merit in Ireland. Many fine houses have been saved through their enthusiasm and commitment, and the dedication of members and supporters. The current President is Desmond FitzGerald, Knight of Glin.

The Society's main achievements include, among others, the saving of threatened great buildings such as: Castletown, Co Kildare; Damer House, Co Tipperary; Doneraile Court, Co Cork; Roundwood, Co Laois; Tailors Hall, Dublin, and 13 Henrietta Street, Dublin. Restoration work is being carried out at Ledwithstown, Co Longford, and Mount Ievers Court, Co Clare, and the Society is assisting with the urban restoration at 2 Pery Square, Limerick. The Society has provided grants for many other projects, including the restoration of correct windows in historic urban houses, such as 20 Lr Dominick Street, George Bernard Shaw's house in Synge Street, and 3-4 Fownes Street, Dublin.

These efforts are funded by our members' participation in the events programme, by the fundraising activities of our chapters, by donations, by sales from the Society's book and gift shop, and by generous royalties from Kindel & Co Inc., Scalamandre Inc., Chelsea House, and the Obelisk Collection.

MEMBERSHIP APPLICATION

Membership application forms are available from:

IRISH GEORGIAN SOCIETY
74 Merrion Square, Dublin 2
tel: +353 (0)1-676 7053 / fax: +353 (0)1-662 0290 / e-mail: igs@iol.ie

Arthur Prager, Executive Director
IRISH GEORGIAN SOCIETY INC.
7 Washington Square North (21A), New York, NY 10003 6647
tel: (212) 254 4862 / fax: (212) 777 6754

If you are an Irish taxpayer, why not become a Contributing (£101) or Life Member (£1,000) of the Irish Georgian Society. You may be eligible for up to 48% tax refund on your contribution. The Irish Georgian Foundation is an approved Artistic Body under Section 32, Finance Act, 1984.

Donations to the Irish Georgian Society Inc., including membership fees, are tax deductible in the US, subject to the tenets of US tax code 1986.

———

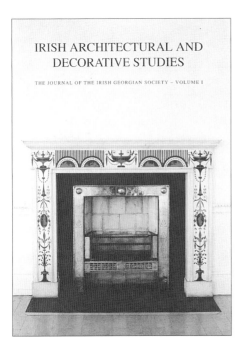

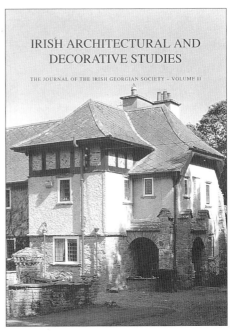

IRISH ARCHITECTURAL AND DECORATIVE STUDIES

THE JOURNAL OF THE IRISH GEORGIAN SOCIETY – VOLUME I, 1998

IRISH ARCHITECTURAL AND DECORATIVE STUDIES

THE JOURNAL OF THE IRISH GEORGIAN SOCIETY – VOLUME II, 2000

Back-issues of IA&DS are available from Irish Georgian Society and Gandon Editions (for contact information, see page 4).